access to history

The Unification of Italy 1789–1896

ROBERT PEARCE AND ANDRINA STILES

FOURTH EDITION

HODDER
EDUCATION
AN HACHETTE UK COMPANY

The Publishers would like to thank Robin Bunce, Nicholas Fellows and Sarah Ward for their contribution to the Study Guide.

The Publishers would like to thank the following for permission to reproduce copyright material:

Photo credits: p28 https://flic.kr/p/oej6xv; **p32** Caricature of Pope Pius IX (1792–1878), 1852 (engraving), Dutch School, (19th century)/Private Collection/Bridgeman Images; **p33** Library of Congress, LC-DIG-pga-01227; **p40** DEA/V. PIROZZI/De Agostini/Getty Images; **p53** Alinari/TopFoto; **p59** https://flic.kr/p/oehYmw; **p63** Library of Congress, LC-USZ62-131393; **p66** Topham Picturepoint; **p70** Topfoto/HIP; **p85** Women stitching red shirts, 1863, by Odoardo Borrani (1834–1905)/De Agostini Picture Library/Bridgeman Images; **p86** Portrait of Giuseppe Garibaldi/De Agostini Picture Library/Bridgeman Images; **p99** Giuseppe Garibaldi (1807–82) injured at the Battle of Aspromonte in 1862 (litho) (b/w photo), Italian School, (19th century)/Musée de la Ville de Paris, Musée Carnavalet, Paris, France/Archives Charmet/Bridgeman Images; **p134** Alessio Nastro Siniscalchi/Attribution-ShareAlike 2.5 Italy (CC BY-SA 2.5 IT).

Acknowledgements: Allen Lane, *The Force of Destiny* by Christopher Duggan, 2007. Barnes & Noble Books, *The Revolutions of 1848–49* by Frank Eyck, 1972. Cooperativa tipografico-editrice P. Galeati, *Scritti Editi ed Inediti* by Giuseppe Mazzini, 1941. Cosimo, *Garibaldi's Defence of the Roman Republic* by George Macaulay Trevelyan, 2008. Feltrinelli, *Stori deli' Italia moderna* by Giorgio Candeloro, 1966. Harper & Row, *Religion from Tolstoy to Camus* by Walter Kaufman, editor, 1964; *The Making of Italy, 1796–1870* by Denis Mack Smith, editor, 1968. Hodder & Stoughton, *The Memoirs of Francesco Crispi*, translated by Mary Pritchard-Agnetti by Thomas Palamnenghi-Crispi, 1912. James S. Virtue, *The Liberators of Italy: Or, the Lives of Garibaldi; Victor Emmanuel, King of Italy; Count Cavour; and Napoleon III, Emperor of the French* by Edward Henry Nolan, 1864. John Murray, *The Roman State: From 1815 to 1850*, translated by W.E. Gladstone by Luigi Carlo Farini, 1851. L. Drummond, *Giuseppe Mazzini: Selected Writings* by Nagendronath Gangulee, editor, 1945. Longman, *The Risorgimento and the Unification of Italy* by Derek Beales, 1981. Macmillan, *The Makers of Modern Italy* by J.A.R. Marriott, 1908. Oliver & Boyd, *The Revolutions of 1848–49* by F. Eyck, editor, 1972. Palgrave Macmillan, *Risorgimento* by Lucy Riall, 2009; *The Making of Italy, 1796–1866* by Denis Mack Smith, 1988. Passigli Editori, *Garibaldi: A Portrait* by Denis Mack Smith, editor, 1982. Prentice-Hall, *Garibaldi* by Dennis Mack Smith, 1969. Princeton University Press, *Garibaldi: Citizen of the World* by Alfonso Scirocco, 2007. Routledge, *The Risorgimento and the Unification of Italy* by Derek Beales and Eugenio F. Biagini, 2014.

Although every effort has been made to ensure that website addresses are correct at time of going to press, Hodder Education cannot be held responsible for the content of any website mentioned in this book. It is sometimes possible to find a relocated web page by typing in the address of the home page for a website in the URL window of your browser.

Hachette UK's policy is to use papers that are natural, renewable and recyclable products and made from wood grown in well-managed forests and other controlled sources. The logging and manufacturing processes are expected to conform to the environmental regulations of the country of origin.

Orders: please contact Hachette UK Distribution, Hely Hutchinson Centre, Milton Road, Didcot, Oxfordshire, OX11 7HH. Telephone: +44 (0)1235 827827. Email education@hachette.co.uk. Lines are open from 9 a.m. to 5 p.m., Monday to Friday. You can also order through our website: www.hoddereducation.com

First published in 1989 by
Hodder Education
An Hachette UK Company
Carmelite House, 50 Victoria Embankment
London EC4Y 0DZ

Impression number   10 9
Year   2022

Cover photo © Mary Evans Picture Library
Produced, illustrated and typeset in Palatino LT Std by Gray Publishing, Tunbridge Wells
Printed and bound by CPI Group (UK) Ltd, Croydon CR0 4YY

A catalogue record for this title is available from the British Library

ISBN 978 1471838590

Contents

Dedication

Keith Randell (1943–2002)

The *Access to History* series was conceived and developed by Keith, who created a series to 'cater for students as they are, not as we might wish them to be'. He leaves a living legacy of a series that for over 20 years has provided a trusted, stimulating and well-loved accompaniment to post-16 study. Our aim with these new editions is to continue to offer students the best possible support for their studies.

CHAPTER 1

Introduction: the unification of Italy

In 1815 'Italy' was merely a geographical expression, and very few people believed that one day the peninsula would become a nation-state. Yet by 1861 almost all of Italy had been unified. This chapter should be regarded as a curtain raiser to the drama of Italian unification, providing essential background knowledge. It looks at three different periods followed by a brief overview:

★ Pre-Napoleonic Italy

★ French rule under Napoleon

★ The Restored Monarchies

★ Unification: a brief overview

Finally, the chapter sketches an outline of the process by which, after 1848, 'Italy' was formed as a political entity, and of the main interpretations that have been put forward by contemporaries and historians to explain what happened. This will allow you to form a 'mental map' of the key events and ideas, enabling you to follow the next, more detailed, chapters with greater ease.

Key dates

1796	Napoleon Bonaparte invaded Italy	**1815**	The 'Restored Monarchs' began to return to their Italian states
1815	Napoleon defeated at Waterloo		
	The Congress of Vienna: Austria to be dominant in Italy	**1859**	Kingdom of Northern Italy formed
		1861	Kingdom of Italy formed

1 Pre-Napoleonic Italy

▶ *What were the main political divisions in Italy?*

Around the start of the nineteenth century, many Europeans considered that Italy was the heartland of world civilisation. Twice, during the Roman Empire and at the time of the Renaissance, it had dominated Europe, first politically and then culturally. Yet the times had sadly changed, and now Italy had declined and was languishing under foreign rule or petty dictators. Italy was now more an art gallery and a museum, some believed, than a modern state.

In 1796, when Napoleon's army had overrun Italy, the peninsula had comprised a complicated patchwork of states and principalities (see the map below). The main bodies of this complex mosaic were (from north to south):

- The northern state of Piedmont was ruled by the House of Savoy from its capital in Turin. In 1720 the Duke of Savoy had acquired the island of Sardinia and the title of King. This joint state had originally been known as 'The Kingdom of Sardinia' or 'Sardinia-Piedmont', but in the nineteenth century was generally referred to simply as Piedmont.
- The northern state of Lombardy was ruled by local representatives of the Austrian Empire, supported by the Austrian army. It was one of the most advanced parts of Italy economically and its capital, Milan, had a population of around 130,000.
- Venetia, governed according to a constitution that had changed little since the Renaissance, was dominated by its local aristocracy. Austria had great influence in the area.

? What does the map tell us about the dominance of Austria in the Italian peninsula?

Figure 1.1 Italy in c.1796, showing the main regions.

- The Central Duchies, of Tuscany, Modena and Parma, were governed by their own dukes, but again Austria was very influential, so much so that they have been called **satellites** of Austria. The ruling dynasty in Tuscany, for instance, the House of Lorraine, was part of the Habsburg family, which ruled in Austria.
- The Papal States, covering most of central Italy, were governed by the Pope. Economically the region was weak, and militarily it relied on support from other Catholic countries.
- The Kingdom of Naples, ruled by the Bourbon family, constituted the largest but also the poorest region in Italy. From Naples, the largest city in Italy, the king also ruled Sicily, which was poverty stricken, via a **viceroy**. The combined kingdom was often referred to as 'The Kingdom of the two Sicilies'.

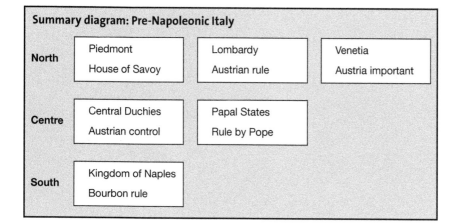

Summary diagram: Pre-Napoleonic Italy

North	Piedmont / House of Savoy	Lombardy / Austrian rule	Venetia / Austria important
Centre	Central Duchies / Austrian control	Papal States / Rule by Pope	
South	Kingdom of Naples / Bourbon rule		

2 French rule under Napoleon

> ▶ *What were the main effects of French rule in Italy?*
> ▶ *What were the positive and what were the negative features of French rule in Italy?*

The French attacked the Kingdom of Piedmont-Sardinia in 1792, acquiring Nice and Savoy. A few years later, in 1796, **Napoleon Bonaparte** gained control of the French army in Italy and, after a war with the Austrians in Lombardy, soon took over the whole peninsula. In 1805 Napoleon crowned himself King of Italy.

Napoleon made a series of changes which simplified political boundaries. In 1798 he did away with the old complicated pattern of states and divided most of the country into just four separate republics. In 1810 he divided the country again, but this time into just three parts (see the map on page 4):

(see the map on page 4)

KEY TERMS

Satellites Weak states dependent on or controlled by a more powerful country.

Viceroy A ruler exercising authority on behalf of a king or queen.

KEY FIGURE

Napoleon Bonaparte (1769–1821)

Joined the French army in 1785 and made a name for himself as a brilliant commander in wars against the British and the Austrians. He instituted a military dictatorship in France in 1799, effectively ending the French Revolution, and crowned himself Emperor, as Napoleon I, in 1804. He was forced to abdicate, after a series of military defeats, in 1814.

? In what ways does this
map differ from that on
page 2?

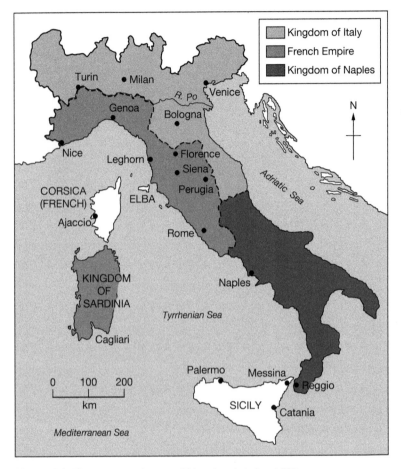

Figure 1.2 The tripartite division of Napoleonic Italy c.1810.

- One-third was annexed to France and treated as part of the French Empire.
  This comprised the north-west portion of Italy, including Piedmont, together
  with the Central Duchies and the Papal States.
- Another third became known as the Kingdom of Italy. This comprised the
  regions of Lombardy, Modena, Bologna, Romagna and Ferrara. Napoleon
  was king but his stepson ruled as viceroy.
- The remaining third was the Kingdom of Naples, but it did not include Sicily,
  which was now controlled by Britain; and the ruling dynasty in Naples was
  no longer the Bourbons. Instead, Napoleon's brother, Joseph, became king.

Life under French rule

Historians are very divided over what life was like for the Italian people under
French rule, not surprisingly perhaps, since almost 20 million people then lived
in the Italian peninsula. Some believe that 'Italy's experience during the period
was traumatic from every point of view' and that the 'brutality and irreligion of
the French soldiery' were largely to blame. Certainly, a great many men were

required for the French army and a great deal of money was needed to train, equip and feed the French soldiers and the Italian conscripts. No fewer than 27,000 Italian soldiers accompanied Napoleon to Russia in 1812, but only 1000, many of them badly wounded, survived to return home on foot, having lost all their horses and cannon in the campaign.

Italians deeply resented the increased conscription of their young men into the army, along with the high taxation needed to make good the loss of so many soldiers, horses and weapons. War, though, was Napoleon's life and as much as 60 per cent of tax revenue collected in Italy by the French authorities was used to fund military expenditure even in peacetime. Nevertheless, the experiences of different groups in Italy undoubtedly varied, as we can see by examining different sectors of Italian society under French rule.

The Church

The Roman Catholic Church was one body that suffered severely. Its power was greatly reduced and two Popes were actually imprisoned in France. In 1809 its **temporal power** was declared to be at an end. The Papal States were to be governed by the French and not by the Pope and his cardinals. This did not affect the Pope's **spiritual authority**, for he remained head of the Church, but by 1814 almost all monasteries had been closed down by the French. In addition, the Church's lands were sold off – and not in the small lots the peasants hoped for and might have been able to buy, but in large lots to landowning noble families or to wealthy merchants from the towns who wanted to set up as landed gentry.

The wealthy

Whether the families of well-to-do noble landowners and of middle-class bankers and merchants suffered under French rule is unclear. Accounts vary widely, but many were written as memoirs long after the events they describe and so may not be entirely accurate. The families of two noblemen who later became prime ministers of Piedmont, Camillo Cavour and Massimo d'Azeglio, are good examples. The Cavours seem to have done well out of the purchase of Church lands, while d'Azeglio, in memoirs written nearly half a century later, complained that his family was ruined under French rule.

Urban groups

There were substantial benefits from French rule for most of the ten per cent or so of Italians who lived in towns. The majority of these were professional men and their families – well-to-do middle-class merchants, lawyers, bankers, apothecaries, doctors and government officials. Lower in the social scale, tradesmen, artisans and craftsmen also profited from the increased prosperity of the middle class as changes introduced by Napoleon brought financial and business advantages.

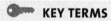 **KEY TERMS**

Temporal power
The worldly authority of the Pope, as ruler of the Papal States.

Spiritual authority
The religious power of the Pope, as head of the Catholic Church.

External customs barriers were simplified and internal trade barriers between the Italian states were swept away, weights and measures were standardised, tax collection was reorganised, new and better roads were built and transport was improved. The **Code Napoléon** was introduced nationally to replace the earlier hotchpotch of separate state laws, and new local government districts were set up along French lines. Industry was encouraged (so that France might benefit from buying cheap Italian goods) and vaccination against smallpox was made available. Street lighting in towns was introduced. At first this caused unexpected problems. It seems that in Milan this new attempt to make the streets safer at night was not appreciated: the flickering oil lamps are said to have 'quite blinded the pedestrians', making them easier targets for pickpockets and other criminals. But in the long run there were undoubted benefits.

The most important development for the future was probably the introduction by the French of a two-chamber representative government in each of the states. Many young Italian men were able to gain experience of politics and government in these 'parliaments'. In addition, Italians absorbed French ideals of liberty, equality and fraternity, and some accepted that men should be citizens of a state rather than subjects of a king. Others were trained in leadership as officers in the French army of occupation or in the **conscripted**, well-trained Italian army of 80,000 men. These experiences were to stand both groups in good stead in the years of revolution and nationalist struggle that were to come.

The peasants

Meanwhile, peasant families, who made up between 80 and 90 per cent of Italians in the early nineteenth century, continued to live a life far removed from that of the **elite** middle-class families of Piedmont or Tuscany, or the old aristocracy of southern Italy. Italian peasant families, ignored in their lifetime and long dismissed by historians as uneducated, unimportant, non-political and unworthy of study, have over the past few decades been the focus of new research.

Marriage customs

The modern-day Italian historian Marzio Barbagli has made an intensive study of the ages at which men and women married within the peasant communities in different parts of Italy and whether they set up their own home or lived with parents. In the rural south, Italian couples married comparatively young, women on average at nineteen years of age and men shortly before they were 25. They were able to do this because the parents of a girl about to marry often supplied her with '**dowry** gifts', including a bed, clothes and linen. Where the families were too poor this was usually impossible. Nevertheless, a landless labourer would often marry and set up a household 'with a few pence of his own, a few from his wife and whatever he can borrow and at once start a family'.

In Sardinia, because her father did not give a dowry, a girl had to make with her own hands the things she needed. As she had very little time during the day, the work took a long while to complete and the age at which she was free to marry was consequently higher than elsewhere. Many young men were never able to marry at all because it was customary in some areas that the head of the family must remain a bachelor.

Occupations

Most peasants lived as they had always done, in dark, damp, poorly furnished cottages that they shared with their livestock for warmth at night. They tilled their fields with wooden ploughs, perhaps with the help of a horse, perhaps not, and carried their crops home on their backs, since over most of rural Italy a wheeled cart was unknown. Unfortunately, the most easily and therefore most commonly grown crop was maize. When eaten in large quantities as the staple diet it results in vitamin deficiency and gives rise to the terrible disease **pellagra**. In one year in the early nineteenth century 95,000 cases were reported among peasants in Venetia alone. The disease affected the poor in north Italy from the end of the eighteenth century to the First World War. The solution was political – with the cultivation and importation of wheat – but its sufferers inevitably took little interest in politics.

Rather than remain almost permanently on the verge of starvation and the prey of bad weather and failed crops, many young men left the family farms, took to the hills and became bandits. Many young women moved for work into the town, where they often found instead diseases such as typhoid, cholera, diphtheria and tuberculosis spread by overcrowding, with as many as 80 people in a house, a non-existent sewerage system and a lack of clean drinking water.

Many women in both town and country discovered, if they did manage to find a job or to obtain work which could be done at home, that it was impossible to keep their babies and often abandoned them at the nearest **foundling** hospital. There a container set in the front door allowed a baby to be left with some sort of identification. If conditions improved, the mother might return and reclaim her child at a later date, months or sometimes years later. By then, however, the child might no longer be alive, for the death rate in foundling hospitals was high.

If peasant women remained in the countryside, they were expected not only to help their husbands in the fields and to feed and care for their families, but also to make a little money at home. Often they would become **outworkers** for some urban merchant by spinning or weaving, sewing shirts or, with the help of the children, raising silk worms and reeling off the silk from the resulting cocoons for the major Italian manufacturing industry of silk weaving.

Conclusion

The effects of French rule in Italy were paradoxical. Many educated Italians were inspired by the ideas the French brought with them, some wanting to imitate France by modernising Italy and even founding an Italian nation-state. On the other hand, French rule all too often fell lamentably short of the standards it

KEY TERMS

Pellagra A disease causing skin complaints, diarrhoea, self-mutilation and madness that often ends in suicide.

Foundling An infant abandoned by its mother and cared for by others.

Outworkers Those provided with work by a factory but doing it at home.

aspired to. Heavy-handed French imperialism inspired a wish in many Italians to overthrow French domination. The question was, could this be achieved? If so, would it be done by peaceful methods, including debate and agreement, or would violence be needed?

Research on the Italian peasantry has revealed that historians' focus on 'high politics' and on the process that led to unification can easily mislead us into thinking that this preoccupied most Italians. But such was certainly not the case. For most Italians life was a constant struggle for survival, and politics seemed entirely irrelevant. Two key questions arise from this:

- Could nationalists mobilise the peasant masses to take an interest in unification? If so, nationalism might well develop into a force to be reckoned with.
- Could politicians – either before or after unification – take the constructive measures that would raise the standard of living for ordinary Italians? If not, a true democracy was unlikely to evolve.

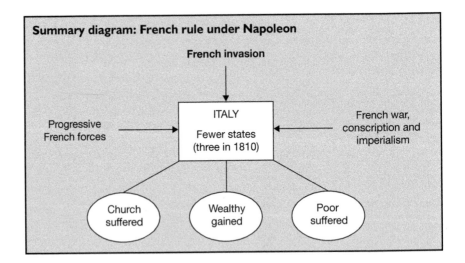

Summary diagram: French rule under Napoleon

3 The Restored Monarchies

▶ *Was life for Italians better or worse under the Restored Monarchs than under the French?*

▶ *Did life for Italians change under the Restored Monarchs?*

In 1815 French control of Italy came to an end with the defeat of Napoleon at Waterloo and his final exile to St Helena. All his boundary changes were set aside. The European powers, meeting at the Congress of Vienna, decided to return Italian state boundaries to more or less what they had been in the middle of the eighteenth century, before Napoleon's arrival.

The main divisions of Italy would be as follows (see the map below):

- In the north, Piedmont was restored to its king, Victor Emmanuel I. His territory was now enlarged to include Savoy, recovered from France, and also **Genoa**.
- Elsewhere in the north, Lombardy and Venetia were now joined together, under a new viceroy controlled from Vienna.
- The Central Duchies (Tuscany, Modena and Parma) were returned to the control of Austrian-appointed local rulers. For instance, Ferdinand III, the brother of the Austrian emperor, became the Grand Duke of Tuscany.
- The Papal States were returned to the control of the Pope, although now Austrian armed forces were to be stationed there.
- In the south, King Ferdinand I was restored to the throne, controlling both Naples and Sicily. He was in theory independent, but he accepted that no important change would be made to his government without Austria's approval.

 **KEY TERM**

Genoa The Vienna Settlement of 1815 gave Piedmont control of the former republic of Genoa. This was of great commercial benefit to Piedmont, as Genoa was an important port. But the Genoese were far from impressed, resenting the loss of their former political and commercial independence.

To what extent did the Congress of Vienna restore the political boundaries of 1796?

Figure 1.3 Italy after the Congress of Vienna 1815.

Prince Clemens Metternich (1773–1859)
The dominant figure in the Austrian government from 1809 to 1848. He was determined to suppress liberal and nationalist movements and regarded dominance in Italy as essential to Austria's security.

Restored Monarchs
The rulers whom the Congress of Vienna allowed to return to Italy.

Reactionary Favouring a return to previous political conditions and being opposed to political progress.

Revisionist historians
Those who disagree with generally accepted historical interpretations and seek to overturn them by arguing differently.

What all this amounted to was an Italy largely controlled by Austria, as the Congress of Vienna had intended. The Congress had decided that, after a period of upheaval, stability was needed. That meant a return to the old ways. Above all, future French invasions had to be prevented, and that meant Austria must control most of the peninsula. This was very much in accordance with the plans of the Austrian chancellor, **Metternich**, one of the key figures in the Congress. He wished 'to extinguish the spirit of Italian unity and ideas about constitutions'. As he said at the time, 'Italian affairs do not exist'.

Old rulers return

In 1815 the old ruling families were clamouring to be allowed to return to Italy from the exile in which most of them had lived out the Napoleonic era. They were anxious, now that their old state boundaries had been restored, to return to their previous lifestyles. It was not long before kings, princes, dukes and duchesses were finding their way back to Italy.

Their return was generally welcomed by the landowning nobility of the countryside, by the well-to-do middle class in the towns and, especially, by the Pope and the Roman Catholic Church. For all these it signalled a welcome return to the old ways.

Yet with very few exceptions the peasants, who made up over 80 per cent of the population, neither knew nor cared what was happening outside their own villages. Whether it was the French, the Austrians or a Restored Monarch who ruled was of little or no importance to them in their struggle for survival.

Life under the Restored Monarchs

The **Restored Monarchs** have long been seen by historians as trying to turn the clock back to pre-Napoleonic times in an attempt to return to absolute government. Hence, they have been judged as essentially **reactionary**. Their alliance with the Church, and also their general friendliness with the Habsburg government in Austria, has led historians to write off the Restored Monarchs as old-fashioned and unprogressive.

Until quite recently the social disturbances and revolutions that took place between 1815 and 1861, when Italy was unified, were described by historians as a struggle between progress (working to make Italy a united independent nation, often through membership of secret societies) and reaction (out-of-date absolute rule, brutal oppression and a general opposition to popular nationalist ambitions for Italian unity and independence).

New research by **revisionist historians**, however, suggests a different situation. They argue that in only a few states did Restoration governments behave in a reactionary way. Most of the opposition, revisionists say, came not because popular demands for a part in government were being ignored: the real trouble was just the opposite. It was not because monarchs were keeping too much power in their own hands, but because they were modernising their governments and setting up a central administration to carry out everyday business. Admittedly, most Restoration governments used censorship, police surveillance and military force to deal with unrest, but so did most other European states in the early nineteenth century.

Examples of **progressive** Restoration governments include the following:

- In Tuscany, Ferdinand III was no reactionary. He improved education, reorganising the universities of Pisa and Siena and spending more on the education of girls. He also expanded health facilities and refused to allow the **Jesuits** entry to the Duchy. Above all, he allowed freedom of expression to a degree not seen elsewhere in Italy. Hence *Antologia*, a monthly journal of literature, arts and sciences, founded in 1821, began to flourish. Its contributors included some of the great intellectual figures of the century, including the leading Italian nationalist, Giuseppe Mazzini. As a result, Florence became, in most people's judgement, the cultural and in some ways the political centre of Italy. Ferdinand would probably have granted a constitution if Metternich had allowed him.
- In Parma, Duchess Marie-Louise was, by the standards of the time, another enlightened ruler. She repealed the *Code Napoléon* (see page 6) but replaced it with something very similar, and she would allow no policy of blind reaction.

There were, however, four states that were indeed backward looking: Piedmont, Modena, the Papal States and Naples.

Piedmont

When King Victor Emanuel I returned to Piedmont in 1815 he set out to turn the clock back to pre-Napoleonic days. Middle-class officials in the government and law courts, and non-noble officers in the army who had been appointed under Napoleon, were dismissed and replaced by members of the old noble families. In addition, the *Code Napoléon* was done away with and the former eighteenth-century laws, with their special privileges for the nobility, were restored. The king even went to the lengths of ploughing up parks and tearing down gaslights because they had been introduced by the French.

The old customs barriers were reintroduced, the use of the new roads built by the French was actively discouraged, control of education was handed back to the Roman Catholic Church, and the Jesuits, who had been exiled by Napoleon, were invited to return. Nobles were given back their lands and, at the same time, the old anti-Jewish laws restricting ownership of property were reintroduced and Jewish people were once again ordered to remain in the **ghettos** instead of being allowed to move freely about the country.

KEY TERMS

Progressive Forward-looking, favouring reform.

Jesuits Members of the Society of Jesus, a religious order founded in the sixteenth century, who were feared for their complete loyalty to the Papacy.

Ghettos Special quarters in Italian towns where Jewish communities were forced to live.

Modena

The return of the Habsburg Duke Francis IV to Modena in 1815 heralded a similar attempt to return to the pre-Napoleonic era. Italians holding government offices under Napoleon were removed, being replaced by members of the nobility. The Jesuits returned. Francis married the daughter of Victor Emmanuel of Piedmont, a man whose rule he much admired. He hated all **liberals**, and yet he also had quarrels with Austria, which confined his rule to the small duchy of Modena.

The Papal States

A series of hard-line Popes, known collectively as 'the zealots', between them established a tight hold on government, education, culture and politics within the Papal States.

All central and local government was in the hands of priests, the **lay population** having almost no say in what happened. The *Code Napoléon* was abolished, censorship was strictly imposed and all opposition forcibly repressed. The **Inquisition** sometimes used torture against those whose ideas were deemed too modern. It was even forbidden to say that the earth revolved round the sun, since the Church decreed otherwise! Religious persecution increased, and toleration of any other belief than Roman Catholic doctrine was forbidden.

Jewish people in particular, came in for harsh treatment. Their children could be taken away to be brought up as Catholics by the Church if it could be shown, or sometimes even if it was alleged, that anyone – a friend, a servant or a relative – had baptised them secretly. The seizing from his home in the ghetto, in 1858, of a young Jewish boy, Edgar Mortara, who may or may not have been baptised by a simple-minded servant girl, created a great sensation which helped, despite the opposition of the Pope, to bring the practice of kidnapping to an end.

Developments in communication were hindered by the Pope's refusal to allow railways and the telegraph within his lands. Economic growth was also hindered.

In this period, the Papal States had the unenviable reputation of being the most backward and oppressive of all the Italian states. They were also among the most economically poor, with unemployment and begging being common.

Naples

The Bourbon king, Ferdinand I, returned as King of Naples in 1815. The following year he cancelled the Sicilian constitution of 1812, which had allowed the people a say in government. In future, he declared, Sicily would be governed as part of the kingdom of Naples. Liberals and **radicals** joined together to call for a new constitution, but the king refused their demand.

In Naples too, Ferdinand's rule was oppressive, cruel and reactionary, and there were very few economic successes that perhaps might have compensated for the stifling political atmosphere. In 1820, in Naples and Sicily, there began the first of a long, drawn-out series of revolutions (which are dealt with in Chapter 2).

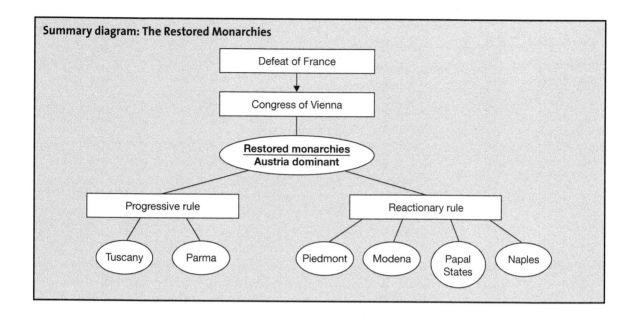

Summary diagram: The Restored Monarchies

```
                    ┌─────────────────────┐
                    │  Defeat of France   │
                    └─────────────────────┘
                              │
                              ▼
                    ┌─────────────────────┐
                    │  Congress of Vienna │
                    └─────────────────────┘
                              │
                    ╭─────────────────────╮
                    │ Restored monarchies │
                    │  Austria dominant   │
                    ╰─────────────────────╯
                     /                   \
          ┌──────────────────┐      ┌──────────────────┐
          │ Progressive rule │      │ Reactionary rule │
          └──────────────────┘      └──────────────────┘
           /          \              /      |      |       \
      Tuscany      Parma        Piedmont  Modena  Papal    Naples
                                                  States
```

 # Unification: a brief overview

▶ *What were the basic 'ingredients' that produced unification?*

▶ *Why did nationalism grow in nineteenth-century Italy?*

Napoleon had said, 'Italy is one nation. Unity of customs, language and literature must at a period more or less distant unite her inhabitants under one government, and Rome without doubt will be chosen by the Italians as their capital'.

In the early 1800s this scenario was only a dream for Italian nationalists. Yet by the 1860s the dream had come true. How it happened is the subject of the rest of this book.

Nationalism

Several factors were involved in the process of unification. One was the growth of national feeling. In the period after French rule, intellectuals became more interested in Italian history and culture, gaining more confidence that Italians were in fact a cultural nation. Philosophers decided around this time that language embodied the distinctive essence of a national group – the special spirit that bound people together and made them a nation, distinct from outsiders. Admittedly, there was no single Italian language, but neither was there quite the linguistic variety in the Italian peninsula that some have believed. Instead, the variations were **dialects** rather than entirely new languages. In addition, one of these dialects – Tuscan Italian – was easily the

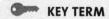 **KEY TERM**

Dialect The form of a language found in a particular region.

KEY FIGURE

Dante Alighieri (1265–1321)

Italian poet. The author of the *Divine Comedy*, he was described by his first biographer as 'that singular splendour of the Italian race'.

most popular form of written language, the one popularised and some said perfected by several key literary figures, including **Dante**.

Yet several important issues were unresolved, all relating to the strength of Italian nationalism:

- Could local discontent, especially with the existing rulers, be converted into enthusiasm for a new Italian state?
- Could Italian nationalism override loyalty to a particular region or state?
- Just how much mass support could Italian nationalism generate? Would it involve only the small intellectual elite, or would it receive support from industrial workers and peasants? The latter constituted the great majority of Italian people, and nationalism would be all the weaker if it could not generate truly mass support.
- How many nationalist parties and groups would there be, and what would they stand for? Should a new Italian state be a republic or a monarchy? Clearly, the more alternatives there were, the less cohesion and the less strength the nationalist movement would have. Unless there was unity, there could be no real strength.
- Would nationalism be strong enough to overcome the existing, mostly Austrian, rulers in Italy, or would the Italians need to enlist international support to overcome the stranglehold of Austria on the Italian peninsula?

Revolutions

Three sets of revolutions occurred in Italy: in 1820–1, 1831–2 and 1848–9. The demands of the rebels in 1820 and 1831 were moderate protests against oppressive rule rather than attempts to forge an Italian nation. They also failed totally, owing to divisions among themselves, lack of mass support and the might of the Austrian army. But in 1848 there was initial success, as the existing rulers often fled their territories. There was also a nationalist aspect to the revolutions. A republic was set up by nationalists in Rome, and Charles Albert, the King of Piedmont – the one ruler in Italy who was definitely an Italian – declared war on Austria and called for independence for an Italian Union. Some believed that the Pope might be made head of a federation of Italian states.

Yet these hopes were soon dashed. French forces restored papal rule in Rome, and the Austrians defeated Piedmontese forces on the battlefield. It was becoming clear that nationalist movements were too weak and too divided among themselves, and that allies were needed to overcome Austrian control. It was also becoming clear that it was the hitherto politically backward state of Piedmont that had the best chance of spearheading the unification of Italy.

Piedmont and unification

Piedmont, under its king, Victor Emmanuel II, and its prime minister, Camillo Cavour, grew stronger in the 1850s; and in 1859, having enlisted the help of the French Emperor, Napoleon III, it defeated Austria and formed the Kingdom of Northern Italy. Here was a successful measure of unification, although it was not altogether easy to say whether it was a result of Italian nationalism or Piedmontese imperialism.

The process might have stopped there, as many in the north looked upon the south of the peninsula as a backward and essentially foreign land. But Giuseppe Garibaldi – a swashbuckling military leader who was determined that the whole of Italy should be free and united – successfully wrested both Sicily and Naples from their Austrian king and, in 1860, handed them over to Victor Emmanuel. The Kingdom of Italy was formed in 1861, very much on the model of Piedmont; and soon the rest of the peninsula was added, Venice in 1866 and Rome, which became the new capital, in 1870, both as a result of diplomacy and Prussia's wars.

Interpretations

How do we make sense of the events that comprised Italian unification? One popular explanation has been to stress nationalism, the force of which produced the **Risorgimento**, a revival or awakening in Italy amounting to a national rebirth. This term is sometimes used loosely, as a **synonym** for Italian unification, but, more correctly, it implies a particular interpretation: that Italy came into being not as a result of war and diplomacy and the actions of foreigners but, essentially, as a result of its own growth and the abilities and actions of Italians.

Many writers from the 1860s onwards have favoured the notion of *Risorgimento*, insisting that the timing of unification and the precise form that it took were determined by the exploits of Cavour and Garibaldi, the two greatest heroes of nineteenth-century Italian history. Their successful partnership brought the *Risorgimento* to a glorious conclusion. The essence of this interpretation is that Italians co-operated, and thus earned their own liberation from oppressive rule.

Most modern historians, however, especially from Britain, are far more sceptical. They cannot see the nationalist movement proceeding to an almost preordained and glorious unification, especially since the new Kingdom of Italy performed badly after 1861 –with political weaknesses, economic backwardness and foreign policy failures – and indeed succumbed to Mussolini's Fascist movement in the 1920s. They note continued divisions between the different nationalist groups during the 1850s and 1860s, as well as the necessity for foreign, especially French, help in defeating Austria, and they tend to see the unification of 1860 stemming not from the co-operation of Cavour and Garibaldi but from their rivalries and indeed hostility. In short, they emphasise **contingent** factors more than those Italian historians who still believe that the *Risorgimento* explains unification.

KEY TERMS

Risorgimento The word first came into use at the end of the eighteenth century and means 'resurgence' or 'rebirth'. Those who first used it suggested that Italian unification would be a noble and heroic affair, paralleling glorious episodes in Italian history such as the Roman Empire and the Renaissance.

Synonym A word that means the same as another word or phrase.

Contingent Subject to chance and to the effects of the unforeseen.

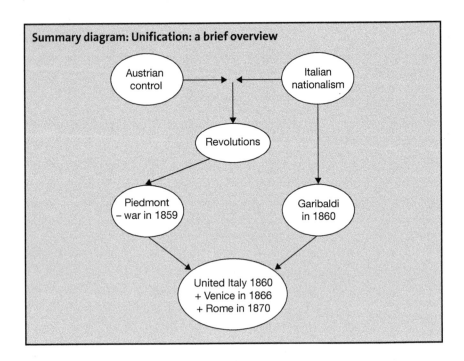

Summary diagram: Unification: a brief overview

Austrian control → ← Italian nationalism → Revolutions → Piedmont – war in 1859 / Garibaldi in 1860 → United Italy 1860 + Venice in 1866 + Rome in 1870

Chapter summary

The French occupation of Italy from 1796 to 1814 boosted Italian nationalism in two ways: it provided Italians with ideals of nationhood and representative government, and it also produced grievances that encouraged Italians to combine against Napoleonic rule. Yet the postwar peace settlement of 1815 restored prewar boundaries in Italy and also restored Austria to its dominant position. There seemed little hope of Italian unification, especially since Italian nationalists were divided among themselves and lacked not only mass support but also foreign military backing. A series of failed revolutions, culminating in 1848, only emphasised the unrealism of nationalist ideals. Yet the growth of Piedmont, support from the French Emperor Napoleon III, and the rivalries of two key Italians, Cavour and Garibaldi, led to the unification of Italy in 1861. Italy had once again come into existence as a single state, though whether this was the glorious rebirth implied by the term *Risorgimento* is open to debate.

Refresher questions

Use these questions to remind yourself of the key material covered in this chapter.

1 What were the main effects of Napoleonic rule on the Italian peninsula?

2 In what ways were the peasants affected by French rule?

3 What was the significance of French rule for nationalist movements in Italy?

4 Why did the Congress of Vienna largely return Italy to its prewar mosaic of states?

5 How ably did the Restored Monarchies govern Italy?

6 How dominant was Austria in Italy from 1815 to 1866?

7 Why did revolutions break out in so many Italian regions in the 1820s, 1830s and 1840s?

8 What were the aims of the liberals and of the radicals?

9 How strong was Italian nationalism in the middle of the nineteenth century?

10 Why was Piedmont so important in the unification of Italy?

11 What is the meaning of the term *Risorgimento*?

12 To what extent did hostility between Cavour and Garibaldi bring about Italian unification?

13 What is the fundamental division between historians on what caused Italian unification?

 ## Question practice

ESSAY QUESTIONS

1 'The period of French domination in Italy from 1796 to 1815 sowed the seeds for later unification.' How far do you agree?

2 Which of the following was the more important in developing Italian nationalism? i) The period of French domination 1796–1815. ii) The period of the Restored Monarchies 1815–48. Explain your answer with reference to both i) and ii).

CHAPTER 2

Risorgimento and revolution 1815–49

This chapter covers a long and important period. It begins by examining:

★ Italian politics in 1815

★ Secret societies

It then focuses on the key events of the period through the following themes:

★ The revolutions of 1820–1

★ The revolutions of 1831–2

★ Giuseppe Mazzini

★ Alternative strategies and leaders

★ The revolutions of 1848–9

★ The Roman Republic and the revolutions of 1848–9

★ Why did the revolutions fail?

Key dates

1820–1		Revolutions	1848	July 24		Charles Albert defeated by Austria at the battle of Custoza
1830	June	Fighting in the streets of Paris led Charles X to abdicate	1849	Feb.		Founding of the Roman Republic
1831		Mazzini founded 'Young Italy'		March 23		Charles Albert defeated at the battle of Novara
1846		Pius IX elected as Pope		June		Ending of the Roman Republic
1848–9		Revolutions				
1848	March 13	The fall of Metternich				

1 Italian politics in 1815

▶ *What political groups existed in Italy after the defeat of Napoleon, and what did each believe?*

▶ *Why did the Austrian chancellor oppose nationalism in Italy?*

There were a number of political groups in Italy in 1815, each having different hopes and aims.

Liberals

Liberals believed that the people had the right to some say in government and that this was best done through a representative assembly, or parliament, elected by property owners. Liberals were also concerned with establishing a rule of law which guaranteed certain rights, such as a fair trial, and certain freedoms, such as free speech for all citizens. They were generally non-violent, mainly middle class and were against both an **absolute monarchy** and a **republican democracy**. They favoured instead a **constitutional monarchy**.

Radicals

Radicals were much more extreme in their views. They wanted social reforms and a fairer distribution of wealth and were often prepared to use violence as a way to obtain their goals. Many of them were members of revolutionary secret societies and believed that political power should lie with the people, not with a parliament unless it were elected by all men and not just by property owners. There was at this time little thought of giving a vote to peasants or to women, since both of these groups were believed to be incapable of taking an intelligent interest in politics. Radicals had many disagreements with the liberals, but at least both groups were opposed to the Restored Monarchies.

Nationalists

Nationalists believed that people of the same race, language, culture and tradition should be united in an independent nation of their own. It should have clear geographical boundaries and not be subject to control by any other nation. Many nationalists went further and wanted a republic instead of a monarchy. Liberals and radicals both supported nationalism and unification as the way forward for Italy, even though they did not agree on whether the means to achieve this aim should be peaceful or violent. There was also widespread disagreement about whether the whole of the Italian peninsula, or merely part of it, should be unified.

Metternich's view

Metternich (see page 10) adopted an entirely negative stance, being totally opposed to nationalism, liberalism and radicalism. He had no intention of allowing such dangerous ideas to spread, as they would undermine not just Austrian control over Italy but perhaps the whole state of Austria, which was not a nation-state but the family property of the Habsburg **dynasty**, containing many different cultural and ethnic groups. Hence, he saw the need to maintain the Italian jigsaw of separate states ruled by absolute monarchs: 'Italy' as a united nation should continue *not* to exist.

In 1815 there were no 'Italians', he insisted, only **Neapolitans**, Piedmontese, Tuscans and the rest, and that was how it should stay. Hence, Italy would be weak, divided and easily controlled by Austria.

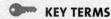

KEY TERMS

Absolute monarchy
A political system under which a monarch rules without a constitution that limits his powers and without a parliament whose agreement is needed for the making of laws.

Republican democracy
A system under which an elected government controls the affairs of a state, and in which there is no monarch, even as a figurehead.

Constitutional monarchy
A system under which a king is bound by certain agreed restrictions on his power set out in a written document (the constitution).

Dynasty A succession of powerful rulers from the same family.

Neapolitans People from Naples.

Metternich was not alone in these beliefs. Many intelligent, well-educated people in Italy saw nothing but difficulties in the way of unity between the Italian states, believing that local loyalties were still more important to the people of the peninsula than dreams of national unity. Hence, the Piedmontese ambassador to Russia wrote about the possible takeover of Genoa by Piedmont in 1818 that perhaps the Piedmontese and the Genoans could not mix, 'separated as they are by ancient and ingrained hatred'.

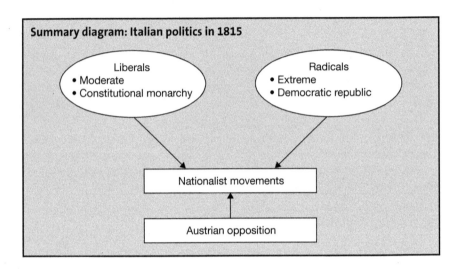

Summary diagram: Italian politics in 1815

Liberals
• Moderate
• Constitutional monarchy

Radicals
• Extreme
• Democratic republic

Nationalist movements

Austrian opposition

2 Secret societies

▶ *What did the secret societies hope to achieve, and why did they have only limited success?*

KEY TERM

Freemasonry A secret fraternity providing fellowship and mutual assistance.

In 1820, when revolutions broke out first in Sicily and then in Naples and Piedmont, secret societies played an important part. These societies are thought to have developed from eighteenth-century **freemasonry** where men formed themselves into groups pledged to mutual protection with secret passwords and semi-religious rituals. The Church viewed these groups with grave suspicion as anti-Catholic and as a danger to the established social order. In the 1790s similar groups, whose main purpose was to drive out the French, had sprung up all over Italy. After 1815 their aims changed to overthrowing the Restored Monarchs and to driving out the Austrians.

Membership

The societies attracted a wide variety of members: army officers, students, lawyers, teachers and doctors, all well educated and mostly middle class. A few noblemen also joined but peasants and workers were almost unknown.

The majority of members were patriotic, enthusiastic and daring. Many were idealists, some were dreamers, a few were rogues and criminals; some wanted to be leaders and were happy to risk their lives in wild adventures and impossible missions.

The great weakness of the societies was their unwillingness to act together and their lack of an overall organisation. Most societies were small and scattered. Sometimes they did work together, but much more often they operated on their own and, because of their emphasis on secrecy, historians are still not sure how many members they had or how successful they were.

The *Carbonari*

Far and away the best known and most important of the societies was the *Carbonari*. They were particularly active in southern Italy, especially in Naples, where they are thought to have had about 60,000 members. This was about five per cent of the adult male population, and the government of Naples became worried enough to order the suppression of the society. Their efforts failed and membership of the *Carbonari* went on rising. It is known that they had elaborate rituals and swore unquestioning obedience to their leaders.

Unlike many of the other societies, this one was not particularly anti-Catholic, and although some of its members planned armed revolution and the overthrow of the existing social order, they were not committed republicans. Often their aims in fact were surprisingly mild ones. In Piedmont they hoped to establish a constitutional monarchy, with a king having only limited power. Similarly, in Naples, they did not want to replace the king with a republic, but just to persuade him to grant a constitution.

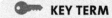 **KEY TERM**

Carbonari From 'charcoal burners' in Italian, and it has been suggested that the earliest members were men who sold charcoal for domestic fuel. Soon, however, middle-class members predominated.

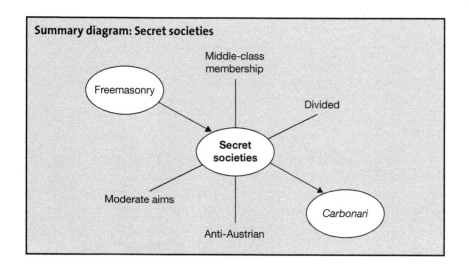

Summary diagram: Secret societies

The revolutions of 1820–1

▶ *Why did the revolutions take place?*

▶ *Why did the revolutions fail?*

Naples

The 1820 revolutions began in Naples where, in 1818, King Ferdinand had greatly increased the Church's power to censor books, newspapers and magazines. This angered the middle class, lawyers and teachers in particular, because freedom of speech was being made impossible. As Ferdinand was short of money he cut back on public spending, halted works such as road and harbour improvements and reduced still further what little education was available to the people. Poverty, corrupt government and restrictions on personal freedom became general.

In January 1820 news of a revolution in Spain encouraged the *Carbonari* and the liberals in Naples to take action. Led by a priest and supported by 100 junior officers and soldiers from the cavalry, 30 *Carbonari* members advanced on the town of Avellino and a widespread uprising soon took place. The attempt by government troops to round up the rebels was very half-hearted, particularly after one of the commanding officers, General **Guglielmo Pepe**, led one infantry and two cavalry regiments to join the rebel army with himself at the head of what had now become a revolution.

In July King Ferdinand promised to meet the rebels' demands for a constitution similar to that granted in Spain in 1812. This had given the vote to all adult males, limited the king's power, and abolished many noble and clerical privileges. King Ferdinand swore to abide by such an arrangement faithfully: 'Omnipotent God – if I lie, do thou at this moment annihilate me.' For a time it looked as if the revolution had been a success, especially when the revolutionaries led by General Pepe marched into the city of Naples and were received by the king. A new government was appointed, Pepe was put in charge of the army and the *Carbonari* gained large numbers of recruits.

Sicily

While all this was going on another and separate revolt had begun in Sicily, the other half of Ferdinand's kingdom, where the people were determined to fight for independence from Naples. Sicily had been forcibly united with Naples in 1815, and Sicilians felt that Ferdinand's government was concentrating on Naples and neglecting their island's needs.

Agricultural prices had fallen sharply, with disastrous consequences for the Sicilian peasants, who found themselves getting more and more into debt. As a result, riots took place in Palermo, the island's capital. There were demands for

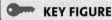 **KEY FIGURE**

Guglielmo Pepe (1783–1855)

Born in southern Italy, he was captured by French forces and fought with distinction for Napoleon. He returned to Italy in 1813 to reorganise the Neapolitan army but switched sides and joined the *Carbonari* when the Bourbons were restored.

a constitution, government offices were burned down, prisoners were released and the Neapolitan governor was sent home by boat as the revolutionaries took over the city.

Failure in Naples and Sicily

In Naples the first meeting of the newly elected parliament took place in October 1820. Its members were middle-class professional men, lawyers, bankers and merchants, along with a few noblemen, some priests, but, of course, no peasants or women. Members discussed what had happened in Sicily and agreed that, at all costs, the island must remain part of the Kingdom of Naples. The island must not be allowed to declare independence and must be brought to heel, by Neapolitan armed force if necessary. Here was a dangerous division of revolutionary forces.

The Austrian chancellor, Metternich, was greatly disturbed that the Neapolitan revolution had apparently been so successful. He did not approve of revolutions – they were unsettling events that disturbed the peace, not only of the state in which they happened, but also in neighbouring states. Therefore, he argued, it was only right for the Great Powers (Austria, Prussia and Russia) to meet and if necessary take action to suppress such disturbances wherever they occurred.

In 1821 the King of Naples was invited to attend one such meeting, at Laibach (modern-day Ljubljana) in Austria. There Ferdinand declared that he had been forced to grant the constitution out of fear and asked for Austria to help him to restore his absolute rule. Metternich did not have to be asked twice. He was delighted to intervene. In March 1821, therefore, the Austrian army entered the city of Naples, despite brave resistance led by General Pepe. Severe reprisals were meted out to the citizens indiscriminately by the Austrian authorities. Arrests, imprisonments and executions became so common that even Metternich was shocked by the savagery and ordered the dismissal of the chief of police.

In Sicily too, the old order was soon in control again. Naples recovered control over Sicily and made a future attempt at breaking away less likely by abolishing the **trade guilds** whose members had been leaders of the revolution there.

Piedmont

Piedmont was the other state that saw revolution erupt in 1820. The king, Victor Emmanuel I, had pursued a very reactionary policy since his return. He declared that the old constitution of 1770 would remain in force and could never be changed. Piedmont would therefore remain an absolute monarchy in spite of continued pressure by a small group of liberals.

When news of what was happening in Naples reached Piedmont, discontent came out into the open. The *Carbonari* rapidly gained new members, and university students, army officers and liberals combined to establish a

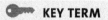

KEY TERM

Trade guilds Associations of craftsmen; early forms of trade unions.

revolutionary government in the town of Alessandria, where they proclaimed their independence as the 'Kingdom of Italy' and declared war on Austria. An army mutiny in Turin, the state capital, encouraged Victor Emmanuel I to see his situation as hopeless and to abdicate.

The liberals now turned for leadership to the young Charles Albert, second in line to the throne. He issued a vague proclamation praising the Spanish constitution of 1812 as a model to be followed, and promptly appointed a new government. The main problem was that he was not the legitimate ruler. Victor Emmanuel's brother, Charles Felix, was first in line to the throne in Piedmont. He was temporarily absent from Piedmont but he soon issued a statement denouncing Charles Albert as a rebel. Charles Felix also refused to accept any change in the form of government. Charles Albert then took fright and fled from Turin, leaving the liberals to fight to defend the constitution as best they could.

At this stage Charles Felix appealed to Metternich for aid. This help came, and Austrian troops, together with troops loyal to Charles Felix, defeated the forces of the Turin liberals at the battle of Novara in 1821. Hundreds of revolutionaries went into exile. The 1820–1 revolutions were over and until 1823 Piedmont was occupied by an Austrian army.

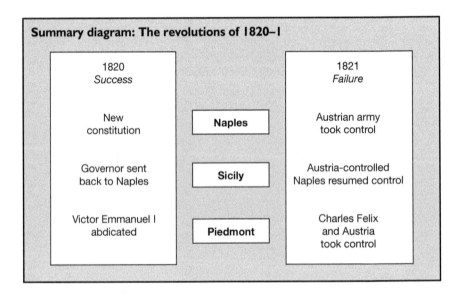

Summary diagram: The revolutions of 1820–1

1820 Success		1821 Failure
New constitution	**Naples**	Austrian army took control
Governor sent back to Naples	**Sicily**	Austria-controlled Naples resumed control
Victor Emmanuel I abdicated	**Piedmont**	Charles Felix and Austria took control

The revolutions of 1831–2

▶ *How far were the revolutions in the early 1830s simply a rerun of those a decade earlier?*

▶ *Why did the revolutions fail in 1820–1 and 1831–2?*

In July 1830 a revolution occurred in Paris. After fierce fighting, in which over 1000 people were killed, the ultra-royalist Charles X was forced to abdicate. The new king, Louis Philippe, was a much more liberal figure than his predecessor; indeed, he was known as the 'citizen king'. Hence, Italian liberals became excited by the possibility that the new French government would support revolutions in Italy. Disturbances broke out again, this time in Modena, Parma and the Papal States. In most of these places the aim was a moderate one – to persuade the local ruler to grant a constitution.

Modena and Parma

In Modena the revolt was led by Enrico Misley, a law graduate and the son of a professor of veterinary science at the University of Milan. He trusted his own ruler, Duke Francis IV of Modena, to whom he revealed his plans for a united Italy, but his trust was betrayed. He was arrested in February 1831, two days before the uprising was due to begin.

Misley's arrest encouraged Duke Francis to believe that the danger was over and he went to Vienna to negotiate for Austrian help, should it be needed on some future occasion. Yet while he was away revolutionaries took over the city of Modena and set up a provisional government. This encouraged students in neighbouring Parma to organise riots and to demand a constitution from their ruler, the Duchess Marie-Louise. She fled in terror and a provisional government was established by the students. Contact with revolutionaries in Modena was at once made and a joint army commander appointed.

Yet the revolutionaries had little time to organise, for within a month Duke Francis had returned to Modena at the head of an Austrian army and quickly defeated the revolutionaries. Savage reprisals were taken and those suspected of supporting the rebels were imprisoned, exiled or executed. Even the wearing of a moustache or beard, supposedly signs of radicalism, could lead men to be arrested as revolutionaries. Parma was also occupied by Austrian forces, and Marie-Louise returned.

The Papal States

Similar uprisings took place in the Papal States, organised this time by the professional classes who resented the oppressive rule of the Church authorities. The papal government put up little resistance and a provisional government known as 'The Government of the Italian Provinces' was formed in Bologna in February 1831. It did not last long. Once more the power of the Austrian army proved decisive: Metternich's troops moved into the Papal States and defeated the rebels. Minor uprisings continued during 1831 and 1832 but they were fiercely suppressed by the often violent and undisciplined Austrian troops.

Revolutionary failure 1820–32

The revolutions of 1820 and 1831 achieved very little. In Piedmont, Naples and the Papal States reactionary governments strengthened their hold with the help of Austria and by using military force.

Where revolutions were successful in ousting their rulers the success was only temporary and due more to the failure of the governments to take effective action, to the rulers' habit of running away and to their lack of military resources than to the strength of the revolutionaries. Remembering what happened in the **French Revolution** at the end of the eighteenth century, many rulers expected to be defeated. This gave the revolutionaries an early advantage, but one that they quickly lost through their failure to take united action. The might of the Austrian army was then brutally decisive.

The revolutions were weakened by being local affairs, concerned only with limited areas. There was little communication between the revolutionaries in the different states and even less co-operation. The revolutionary government in Bologna refused to send help to Modena, for instance. Elsewhere revolutions were not co-ordinated. They relied heavily on a network of small groups of revolutionaries set up by the *Carbonari* and other secret societies, but these were isolated units and their aims differed from place to place. Most revolutionaries were surprisingly moderate in their demands and not given to violence: usually all they were trying to achieve was the granting of a constitution to allow the people some part in government.

The revolutionary movements were mainly middle class, except in Sicily where peasants were involved. Elsewhere popular interest and support were not encouraged by the revolutionary leaders, who feared that allowing the mass of poorly educated people to join in the revolutions would lead eventually to rule by the mob. Not surprisingly, therefore, ordinary people often welcomed back their former rulers with open arms because middle-class revolutionaries did not want their involvement in politics.

In short, the revolutions had failed because the revolutionaries were divided among themselves and lacked mass support, and because they lacked outside help. It was hoped in 1831 that the French might provide military support, but when this was not forthcoming the Austrian army had an easy time of it.

By 1831 Italy was still merely a geographical expression. Unification was not even on the agenda. But what of the future? Would the unsuccessful revolutions of the 1820s and 1830s, and the martyrs that had been created, inspire greater efforts? Could revolutionaries achieve greater unity and greater support? Would the international situation become more favourable?

KEY TERM

French Revolution In the 'great revolution', beginning in 1789, the existing order was overthrown and a republic set up, Louis XVI being executed in 1793.

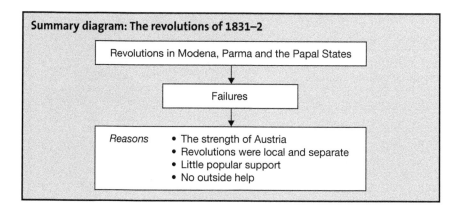

Summary diagram: The revolutions of 1831–2

Revolutions in Modena, Parma and the Papal States

↓

Failures

↓

Reasons
- The strength of Austria
- Revolutions were local and separate
- Little popular support
- No outside help

5 Giuseppe Mazzini

▶ *How important a figure was Mazzini in the movement for Italian unification?*

▶ *What did Mazzini achieve?*

Despite the failure of the revolutions of the early 1830s, it was in this decade that the *Risorgimento* (see page 15) began to make some progress. This was due above all to the work of a dedicated revolutionary intellectual, Giuseppe Mazzini, dubbed by his archenemy Metternich 'the most dangerous man in Europe'.

Mazzini's ideas

It is not easy to get to grips with Mazzini's thought, and few thinkers have been so misunderstood and caricatured. Nevertheless, Denis Mack Smith, in his superb biography (1994), has provided a convincing analysis of his ideas:

- Mazzini took ideas very seriously. 'One cannot execute ideas', he said, adding that they would 'ripen quickly when nourished by the blood of martyrs'.
- He insisted that he had 'one overriding aim' and that was 'the brotherhood of people'. He believed in the equality of human beings and of races. He had contempt for **xenophobia** and imperialism.
- Yet he believed that the next stage of the world's history would be domination by nations. The political map had to be redrawn so that distinct peoples occupied their own nation-states. (This stress on nationalism led **Karl Marx** to dismiss Mazzini as 'that everlasting old ass', but it is a weakness of Marx that he fatally underestimated the importance of national allegiances.)
- So, Italy had to be united.
- He did not want a **federal** Italy, which might retain the old foreign rulers. Instead, the whole peninsula should be independent, with one central government and locally elected authorities.
- There should be democracy and the guarantee of individual rights.

 KEY TERMS

Xenophobia Hatred of foreigners.

Federal Possessing states that are self-governing in their internal affairs.

 KEY FIGURE

Karl Marx (1818–83)
The socialist philosopher and activist who argued that national identities were superficial: the fundamental division among human beings was their class allegiance.

Giuseppe Mazzini

1805	Born in Genoa; intelligent, sensitive and physically frail
1821	Became a nationalist after seeing Piedmontese refugee revolutionaries begging in the streets
1822–7	Studied medicine and then law
1827	Joined the *Carbonari*, but was betrayed in 1830. While imprisoned, he decided he must work for the independence and unification of Italy. He now became a full-time and totally committed revolutionary. He wore black as a sign of mourning for his divided and oppressed country
1831	Moved to the south of France where he founded 'Young Italy' (*La Giovine Italia*), Italy's first real political party
1837	Went into exile in London
1849	Returned to Italy as head of the Roman Republic until Rome fell to the French in June 1849. Again exiled to London where he lived in poverty, writing tens of thousands of letters and hundreds of books and articles
1872	After many years in exile he returned secretly to Italy. Died in Pisa and buried in Genoa, his birthplace

Mazzini was a highly controversial figure. His radical approach led his political enemies to criticise him as an enemy of Italy and a terrorist, and at the same time as a romantic, impractical dreamer. Yet his supporters described him as 'greatest, bravest, most heroic of Italians' and as a profound thinker. Historians' verdicts too have differed widely, partly because his thinking was complex and evolved over a long period and partly because, as an exile often under sentence of death, he often destroyed his letters. (Those that survived were written in handwriting so tiny that it served as a secret code.) What is certain, however, is that he is a key figure in the history of the *Risorgimento* and of Italian unification.

- Italy should be unified by its own efforts. He wanted to avoid help from France, as that might merely replace one form of outside domination by another.
- The ideal was that there should be unification 'from below'. The people should rise up against their oppressors. But if monarchs were prepared to fight against Austrian domination, they should be supported. Mazzini was flexible in his tactics: he was not absolutely committed to republicanism, although this was his ideal.
- Socially, he wanted greater equality, with an end to poverty and with taxation being proportional to wealth. There should be free and compulsory education for all and women's rights should be guaranteed.

Mazzini's ideas constitute a remarkably 'modern' agenda, and a remarkably radical one in the nineteenth century. No wonder moderate liberals in the 1840s looked on him as dangerous. How could they attract the support of France, while he called for all foreign nations to stand aside from Italian affairs? How could they generate support from wealthy figures, while he wished to see a redistribution of wealth? How could they appeal to individual Italian rulers, while his ideal was republicanism? Mazzini might on occasions appeal for the support of particular rulers, but the **ambivalence** of his thought on this issue must surely have made them wary.

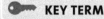 **KEY TERM**

Ambivalence Contradictory ideas or feelings.

Conclusion

Italy was unified, as Mazzini said it would be, and nationalism did indeed prove a potent force in nineteenth- and twentieth-century history. Furthermore, Mazzini's ideas inspired many disciples. Yet history did not follow the exact pattern he desired. As we shall see, Italy came to be unified more 'from above' than 'from below', much to his disgust. He was to describe the new Italian unified state as a 'dead corpse'.

Many may judge that an Italy unified on Mazzinian lines would have been a more liberal, progressive and altogether preferable state to the one that did emerge. Others, however, will think that his ideal state was far too idealised ever to exist.

'Young Italy'

Mazzini was not merely a thinker, he aspired also to be a doer. When Charles Albert finally became King of Piedmont in 1831, Mazzini wrote to him about the coming revolution and invited him to become its leader. 'Put yourself at the head of the nation; write on your banner "Union, Liberty, Independence" … Give your name to a century.' He added privately, 'Not that I have any hopes of him', and he was right. No reply came from Charles Albert. Shortly afterwards Mazzini tried other tactics.

Later in 1831, dissatisfied with the limited progress brought about by the secret societies, Mazzini founded an organisation with much clearer objectives. 'Young Italy' has been called Italy's first real political party. Source A indicates how he described the new party.

SOURCE A

From Mazzini's 'General Instructions for the Members of Young Italy', 1831, quoted in Derek Beales, *The Risorgimento and the Unification of Italy*, Longman, 1981, p. 129.

Young Italy is a brotherhood of Italians who believe in a law of Progress and Duty and are convinced that Italy is destined to become one nation – convinced also that she possesses sufficient strength within herself to become one, and that the ill success of her former efforts is to be attributed not to the weakness, but to the misdirection of the revolutionary elements within her – that the secret of force lies in constancy and unity of effort. They join this association in the firm intent of consecrating both thought and action to the great aim of re-constituting Italy as one independent sovereign nation of free men and equals.

Why may Italians have found the words in Source A inspiring?

Those who joined had to swear to work to make Italy 'one free independent republican nation'. Members would campaign peacefully and attempt to convince others of their views, but Mazzini also accepted that on occasions violent tactics might be necessary.

Soon Mazzini and 'Young Italy' were involved in various attempts to further the cause of unification:

- in a plan for an uprising in Naples in 1832, on the assumption that the peasants were 'a volcano about to erupt'
- in organising a mutiny in the Piedmontese army
- in a rising in Savoy
- in an attempted **coup** in Piedmont, for which, in his absence, he was condemned to death.

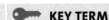

KEY TERM

Coup A sudden and violent seizure of power.

None of these, however, came anywhere near to success. Their main effect was probably to allow Mazzini's political enemies to spread scare stories. Metternich, for instance, insisted – quite inaccurately – that he was trying to assassinate Charles Albert.

Mazzini's significance

Mazzini gave tremendous impetus to Italian nationalism. No one else campaigned for so long or so tirelessly in the cause of a united Italy. He spent most of his time organising a propaganda campaign to convince Italians to support the creation of a democratic, self-governing state of Italy. It is thus as an inspirational prophet that Mazzini's true significance lies. But he has two other claims to fame:

- He 'converted' many to the cause. Easily the most important of his recruits was Giuseppe Garibaldi, who involved himself in a proposed Mazzinian revolt in Genoa in 1831. The scheme failed but Garibaldi escaped before his trial and was sentenced to death in his absence. He recalled of Mazzini that 'he alone was awake when all around were slumbering'.
- Mazzini, whom many considered an impractical dreamer, became, in effect, President of Rome in 1849, and in this position he showed highly constructive abilities (see pages 39–41).

Mazzini's major weakness was that his ideas were too intellectual for most people to grasp, and they were certainly too radical for most cautious, middle-class reformers. He was also absent from Italy for such long periods – totalling in all over 40 years – that he became out of touch with the situation, exaggerating the development of national identity among the bulk of Italians. It is untrue that he failed to appreciate the revolutionary potential of the peasants, but it must be admitted that he knew relatively little about them and had even less contact with them.

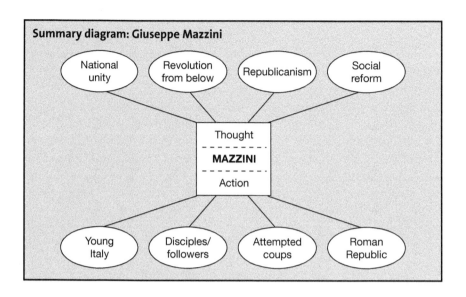

Summary diagram: Giuseppe Mazzini

 6 **Alternative strategies and leaders**

▶ *Why did some believe that Piedmont should lead Italy?*

▶ *Why did Pius IX turn out to be such an unsuitable Italian leader?*

Mazzini was not the only revolutionary leader, and ideas very different from his were circulating among the educated elite. Two strategies focused on Piedmont and on the Pope.

Piedmont

In Piedmont moderate nationalists, taking their lead from **Cesare Balbo**, proposed that their state should lead the other Italian states in an attempt to drive out the Austrians. They argued that only Piedmont was strong enough to reclaim Lombardy and Venetia from the Austrians and rally the other Italian states into some sort of union. Proposals were put forward that Charles Albert should be the future king of a united Italy, although some believed that this new state should cover only the northern half, rather than the whole, of the peninsula.

As we shall see in the next chapter, this strategy achieved a good deal of success, although under Charles Albert's successor as King of Piedmont.

 KEY FIGURE

Cesare Balbo (1789–1853)

Wrote widely on Italian history and politics. His 1844 publication, *On the Hopes of Italy*, argued that Piedmont should spearhead Italian unity.

? How would you describe the facial features of the Pope in Source B?

Pope Pius IX

Another possible leader was suggested by the Piedmontese writer **Vincenzo Gioberti**. In 1843 he suggested that, as the Pope and the Catholic Church were the glories of Italy, the Italian states should form themselves into a federation with the Pope as its president. The bad reputation of the Papal States as oppressive and corrupt seemed too great a stumbling block for his ideas to be put into operation. However, the situation changed in 1846 with the election of a new Pope, Pius IX, who was believed to have liberal sympathies. Many were astounded that such a figure had been elected. 'We were prepared for anything', said Metternich in disbelief, 'except a liberal Pope'.

SOURCE B

In this hostile cartoon from 1852 Pius is depicted as removing the mask of piety to reveal a very different reality underneath.

Pius IX was a man of personal piety and deep faith, but emotional, excitable and with a quick temper. He was seen by many who knew him as impressionable, impulsive and unpredictable. Pius said of himself, in a letter to a previous Pope, that owing to his epilepsy he 'had a very weak memory and could not concentrate on a subject for any length of time without having to worry about

Pope Pius IX

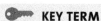

1792   Born as Giovanni Maria Mastai-Ferretti in Ancona, ninth child of a noble family with strong Church connections

1807   Developed epilepsy; entered the Church

1819   Became a priest, progressing to cardinal in 1845

1846   Surprise choice as Pope on the death of Gregory XVI. Took name of Pius IX (known in Italy as Pope *Pio Nono*). Appeared to be liberal

1848   Complete change of policy. Suddenly condemned Italian nationalists, rejected the *Risorgimento* and refused to allow papal troops to help drive out the Austrians. Had to escape in disguise from Rome as revolution began

1849   **Excommunicated** all who tried to reduce temporal power of papacy, and denounced Roman Republic

1850   Returned to Rome. Abolished all early reforms

1861   Catholics forbidden to have any connection with the new Kingdom of Italy

1864   *Syllabus of Errors* published, rejecting liberalism, nationalism and other 'pernicious errors'

1870   First Vatican Council held. Attempt to increase Pope's spiritual power, now that he had lost most of the temporal power. Papal decisions declared infallible. Freedom of religion opposed: Catholic doctrine was the only true belief

1878   Died within a month of Victor Emmanuel II, his long-standing enemy

Pius IX seemed a distinctly 'modern' figure. He was, for instance, the first Pope to be photographed. His reputation for liberalism seemed fully justified in 1846–7. He freed around 2000 political prisoners, mostly revolutionaries; he reformed education, the law and papal administration; and he gave laymen a greater role in public affairs. He also ended press censorship, released Jewish people from of the ghetto, granted Rome a constitution to replace absolute papal rule, and created the *Consulta*, an elected body to advise the Pope. Here, it seemed, was the figure that Gioberti and other nationalists had hoped for. His rapid transformation into the enemy of Italian nationalism, which was a profound blow to liberals in Italy, is extremely hard to explain.

🔑 KEY TERM

Excommunicated Excluded from the services and sacraments of the Catholic Church. Those who died excommunicated could not be buried by a priest or in consecrated ground, and so, it was commonly believed, would go to hell.

---

his ideas getting terribly confused'. He was very easily influenced by stronger personalities and was described by the British ambassador in 1860 as having 'an amiable but weak mind'.

Pius is remembered today for the length of his reign and for his firm stand on Catholic doctrine – and for his amazing transformation on the issue of Italian unification. The man who initially seemed to be a liberal turned out to be a reactionary.

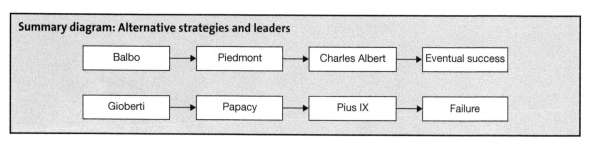

Summary diagram: Alternative strategies and leaders

Balbo → Piedmont → Charles Albert → Eventual success

Gioberti → Papacy → Pius IX → Failure

The revolutions of 1848–9

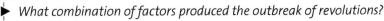

▶ *What combination of factors produced the outbreak of revolutions?*

▶ *How did events in one area of Italy impact on those in others?*

Origins

The Pope's reforms in 1848 and early 1849 set an example to other states and their rulers. In Piedmont and Tuscany, press censorship was abolished and proposals were made for a joint **customs union** with the Papal States. Even Austrian-controlled Lombardy became restless, worrying Metternich, who acted swiftly to preserve Austrian control in northern Italy by making new treaties with Modena and Parma and by strengthening the Austrian **garrison**.

There was now a chorus of discontent in Italy, and it was becoming ever louder. Liberals were calling for constitutions, government reforms and political freedom, while nationalists demanded independence from Austria and some measure of Italian unity.

The situation became more acute owing to economic problems. Almost 90 per cent of the population of Italy worked on the land and the Italian economy was based almost entirely on agriculture. There was little industry in the north and almost none in the south of the country. When the harvests failed in 1846 and 1847, therefore, problems multiplied not only for the peasants but also for those in the towns. Shortages of wheat and maize meant high prices, wages did not rise to meet the increased costs, and peasants and others could not afford to feed their families. Here was a revolutionary situation.

The course of the revolutions

The year 1848 was dominated by revolutions, and not only in Italy. There was revolutionary activity in every major city on the continent of Europe. The two most momentous revolutions occurred in France and Austria. On 24 February, in Paris, an angry mob forced King Louis Philippe to abdicate and flee the country. The following month, in Vienna, crowds successfully called for the dismissal of Metternich, the symbol of resistance to reform. But Italy was certainly not immune to change. Indeed it was here, in Sicily, that the first revolution of 1848 took place.

Success in Sicily

On becoming king in 1830, Ferdinand II of Naples had promised reform: he would, he insisted, govern in a way that promoted the greatest good of the greatest number of his subjects. He even appointed a viceroy to make sure that beneficial reforms were carried out in Sicily. But initial hopes soon foundered, and liberal reforms gave way to repression, and at a time when an outbreak of cholera left Sicilians in a desperate state.

KEY TERMS

Customs union
An economic agreement whereby two or more states agree to lower or eliminate taxes on the goods they trade with each other.

Garrison A body of troops stationed to defend a town or locality.

In January 1848 notices were posted up in Palermo, the island's capital (see Source C).

SOURCE C

From notices posted up in Palermo, quoted in Giorgio Candeloro, *Stori deli' Italia moderna*, second edition, volume III, Feltrinelli, 1966, p. 122.

Sicilians! the time for prayers is past; peaceful protests and demonstrations have all been useless. Ferdinand, King of Naples, has treated them all with contempt and we, as people born free, are loaded with chains and reduced to misery. Shall we still delay claiming our lawful rights? To arms, sons of Sicily; our united force will be invincible …

What were the 'lawful rights' referred to in Source C?

The notices went on to explain that weapons would be handed out to those who came to the main public square at dawn three days later. The authorities could not really believe that a revolution was being announced in advance, but they took no chances and arrested a few likely suspects.

On the day specified, the streets were full of people, but whether they were ordinary sightseers or revolutionaries is impossible to say. After what arms were available had been handed out there were clashes with the government troops. On the following day peasants from outside the city arrived to join in the rising. The Neapolitan army retaliated by shelling the city, and they were joined two days later by 5000 reinforcements. They found that the revolutionaries had successfully taken over the city and were demanding a restoration of the famous 1812 constitution that had been abolished by the King of Naples in 1816 (see page 12). A compromise was offered. It was refused.

Fighting continued and by April the revolutionaries had taken over most of the island. A provisional government was set up with the help of middle-class moderates, who were becoming anxious about what the peasants might do next. A civic guard was formed to control 'the masses' who were marching on towns and villages, destroying property, freeing prisoners and burning tax-collection records. A parliament was elected and it declared that Naples and Sicily were finally totally separated and divided, and that the King of Naples was no longer King of Sicily. The Sicilians' aim was as always, in 1848 as in 1820, to free themselves from Naples. They were not concerned with national unity – quite the opposite. Theirs was a separatist movement with the aim of breaking away from Naples and making Sicily independent.

Failure in Naples and Sicily

On the mainland, the revolution spread to Naples within a few days of the uprising in Palermo. A huge demonstration demanded a constitution. The king agreed to a two-chamber parliament with limited powers. He also agreed to form a national guard and to free the press from censorship. Nevertheless, peasant grievances over their right to use common land led to fighting, and now Ferdinand's troops were successful.

By September 1848 the government in Naples was able to send troops to retake Sicily. The Sicilians were defeated, after an intense bombardment of local towns which earned Ferdinand the nickname 'King Bomba', and by the spring of 1849 they were forced to accept reunification with Naples. There the king had already gone back on his earlier promises, abolished parliament and replaced it with absolute rule and a police state.

Success in central and northern Italy

Serious disturbances were occurring in the rest of Italy as well in 1848. As a result, the Grand Duke of Tuscany and the King of Piedmont promised to grant constitutions. Their example was soon followed by the Pope in the Papal States, while in Modena and Parma the rulers had to leave their states and flee for their lives.

Trouble started in Milan, in Austrian-controlled Lombardy, as a tobacco boycott. Tobacco was an Austrian state monopoly and the people of Milan believed that if they stopped smoking then Austrian finances would be seriously affected. The sight of Austrian soldiers smoking in public was an excuse for attacking them, and small-scale fights quickly turned into larger riots and eventually into a full-scale revolution known as 'The Five Days' (17–22 March). The mayor of Milan, Count Gabrio Casati, arranged for armed men to surround government buildings, and after several guards were shot the vice governor, Count O'Donnell, gave way to the protestors' demands. The commander-in-chief of the Austrian forces in Italy, the 81-year-old General Radetzky (remembered now for the march tune bearing his name composed by Johann Strauss Sr), decided to withdraw from the city, not so much because he was defeated, though he feared the strength of the opposing forces, but because the situation in Austria had changed dramatically. Revolution had broken out in Vienna and Metternich had resigned.

The provisional government set up in Milan by the revolutionaries prepared to continue the fight against Austria. They decided to ask for help from the neighbouring state of Piedmont, whose king, Charles Albert, had just granted a constitution to his people (see page 54). A week later, Charles Albert agreed to declare war on Austria and the provisional government in Milan issued an emotional appeal to their fellow citizens (see Source D).

SOURCE D

? What inaccuracies are contained in Source D?

From an appeal by the provisional government of Milan to its fellow citizens, March 1848, quoted in Frank Eyck, *The Revolutions of 1848–49*, Barnes & Noble Books, 1972, p. 72.

We have conquered. We have compelled the enemy to fly, oppressed as much by his own shame as our valour; but scattered in our fields, wandering like wild beasts, united in bands of plunderers, he prolonged for us the horrors of war without affording any of its sublime emotions. This makes it easy to understand that the arms we have taken up, and still hold, can never be laid down as long as one of his band shall be hid under cover of the Alps. We have sworn, we swear it again, with the generous Prince who flies to associate himself with our glory – all Italy swears it and so it shall be.

To arms then, to arms, to secure the fruits of our glorious revolution – to fight the last battle of independence and the Italian Union.

In the other Austrian-controlled state, Venetia, a small-scale revolt persuaded the Austrians to surrender, and the Independent Venetian Republic of St Mark was proclaimed in March 1849 by **Daniele Manin**. Its rapidly elected assembly voted for union with Piedmont.

The impact of the Pope

At first all went well with Charles Albert. His army defeated the Austrians at the end of May 1848, but in the Papal States things were not going so well. The Pope's army commander had disobeyed orders and set off with his troops to join

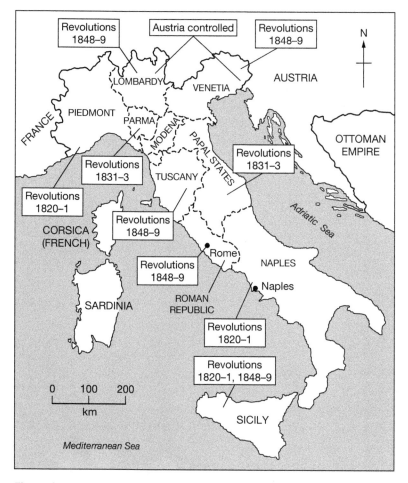

Figure 2.1 Revolutions in Italy 1820–49.

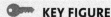 **KEY FIGURE**

Daniele Manin (1804–57)

A Venetian who was arrested in January 1848 for petitioning for reform. In March the people forced the Austrian governor to release him, and he was a key figure in Venice until the Austrians reasserted their control in August 1849.

Why were certain areas of Italy prone to revolution?

Charles Albert's army. This made difficulties for the Pope, who was not at war with Austria. He decided to keep out of the war and, to make his position clear, issued an **allocution** to senior clerics (see Source E).

> ? What reasons does the Pope give for opposing the revolution in Source E?

SOURCE E

From an allocution issued by Pope Pius IX, 29 April 1848, quoted in Luigi Carlo Farini, *The Roman State: From 1815 to 1850*, volume 2, translated by W.E. Gladstone, John Murray, 1851, p. 110.

… Seeing that some at present desire that We too, along with the other Princes of Italy and their subjects, should engage in war against the Austrians, We have thought it convenient to proclaim clearly and openly, in this our solemn Assembly, that such a measure is altogether alien from our counsels … We cannot refrain from repudiating … the treacherous advice, published … in journals, and in various works, of those who want the Roman Pontiff [the Pope] to be the head and to preside over the formation of some sort of novel Republic of the whole Italian people. Rather, on this occasion, … We do urgently warn … the Italian people to abstain with all diligence from the like counsels, deceitful and ruinous to Italy herself, and to abide in close attachment to their respective Sovereigns, of whose good-will they have already had experience, so as never to let themselves be torn away …

KEY TERMS

Allocution An official speech giving a warning or advice.

Anticlerical Unsympathetic or hostile to the Church and its clergy.

Armistice A truce, or ceasefire.

Pius IX made it clear not only that he would not join in the war against Austria, but also that he was no longer interested in the idea of becoming head of an Italian federation of states, or even in the idea of the Church lending support for a united Italy. Two years earlier the Pope had 'blessed "Italy"'. He now withdrew his blessing. The Church had turned its back on liberalism and gone over to the side of reaction and absolutism.

For Charles Albert and other loyal Catholics, the loss of papal support for their cause was a bitter blow. They would now have to choose between following their political principles and obeying their spiritual leader. It was a difficult decision but many decided in favour of their political principles. As a result, the liberal and nationalist movements became noticeably **anticlerical**.

Revolutionary setbacks

The fall of Metternich had not produced any really fundamental change in Austria, and a strong figure emerged – in Sophie of Bavaria – to rally the regime. In December 1848 she had her son crowned as Emperor Franz Joseph, and even before this, in June, after the restoration of calm in Austria, Radetzky arrived back in Italy with reinforcements. In July Radetzky defeated Charles Albert's army at Custoza. An **armistice** was signed and Piedmont withdrew from Lombardy, leaving it in Austrian hands. The Venetians hurriedly cancelled their recently completed union with Piedmont, re-established the former Republic of St Mark and, under Manin and the Neapolitan General Pepe, prepared to continue the war with Austria.

At this moment Mazzini arrived back in Italy after long years of exile. The 'war of the princes' against Austria had failed; now it was time for the 'war of the people'.

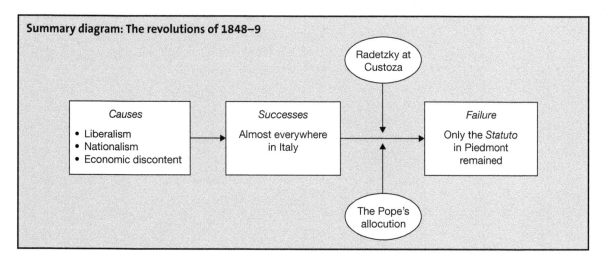

Summary diagram: The revolutions of 1848–9

Causes
- Liberalism
- Nationalism
- Economic discontent

Successes
Almost everywhere in Italy

Radetzky at Custoza

The Pope's allocution

Failure
Only the *Statuto* in Piedmont remained

8 The Roman Republic and the revolutions of 1848–9

▶ *What did the Roman Republic achieve?*
▶ *Why did revolutions continue to fail in 1848–9?*

The Pope flees

In Rome the Pope's unpopular chief minister, Count Pellegrino Rossi, was murdered at the end of November 1848. Rioting followed and the Pope fled from a city in turmoil to take refuge in Naples, while the government that he had left behind announced a series of reforms. It abolished the unpopular tax on grinding corn, provided public building work for unemployed people and proposed the holding of a **Constituente**. The election of these representatives was organised by a special Council of State whose members were chosen by the government of Rome, and the *Constituente* met for the first time in February 1849. Among its members was Garibaldi. Four days later the *Constituente* proclaimed an end to the temporal power of the Pope and the establishment of the Roman Republic.

Mazzini's Roman Republic

In March Mazzini arrived in Rome and was elected as head of a **triumvirate** (see the illustration on page 40) that would rule the city. In fact, though, Mazzini did most of the work and made most of the decisions himself.

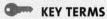
KEY TERMS

Constituente A meeting in Rome of representatives from all over Italy.

Triumvirate A governing group of three men.

During the 100 days of his power, Mazzini had to deal with a difficult situation, especially as the rich had fled the city, unemployment had risen and his enemies outside Rome were spreading rumours that he was being wantonly cruel and burning people alive. But he governed in a fair, tolerant and enlightened way:

- He abolished the death penalty and the Inquisition.
- Taxation was reformed to aid the poor.
- The clerical monopoly on education was ended.
- A dozen new newspapers started up.
- He declared Catholicism to be the official religion of the new republic, as a majority of its inhabitants wanted.
- He also urged that Rome, Piedmont, Florence and Venice should work together to end Austrian rule in Italy.

Mazzini was described by an American observer in Rome as 'a man of genius, an elevated thinker … the only great Italian … in action as decisive and full of resource as Caesar'.

The republic did not last long enough for the real effects of his actions to become clear, but many Romans took inspiration from these months and remembered them for a long time to come.

The fall of the republic

The Pope appealed to France, Spain and Naples to help free Rome 'from the enemies of our most holy religion and civil society', and an army of about 20,000 men was sent from France to destroy the Roman Republic. (For further details, see pages 88–9.) This they did, for although the gallant defence of the city by Garibaldi became one of the legends of the *Risorgimento*, the odds against him were too great and the city fell to the French at the end of June 1849. A French garrison with the duty of safeguarding the Pope remained in Rome until 1870.

SOURCE F

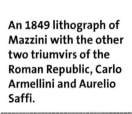

Why do you think Mazzini is given such prominence in Source F, being positioned head and shoulders above the other two?

An 1849 lithograph of Mazzini with the other two triumvirs of the Roman Republic, Carlo Armellini and Aurelio Saffi.

Mazzini explained why the Roman Republic fought so fiercely (see Source G).

SOURCE G

From Mazzini's explanation of why the Roman Republic fought so fiercely, quoted in George Macaulay Trevelyan, *Garibaldi's Defence of the Roman Republic*, Cosimo, 2008, p. 112.

To the many other causes which decided us to resist, there was one closely bound up with the aim of my whole life – the foundation of a national unity. Rome was the natural centre of that unity and it was important to attract the eyes and reverence of my countrymen towards her … It was essential to redeem Rome; to place her once again at the summit so that Italians might again learn to regard her as the temple of their common country …

What elements of romanticism are contained in Source G?

After the fall of the city, Mazzini was downhearted but still optimistic. He appealed to citizens (see Source H).

SOURCE H

A message to the people of Rome from Mazzini after the Roman Republic was defeated by the French in June 1849, quoted in Nagendronath Gangulee, editor, *Giuseppe Mazzini: Selected Writings*, L. Drummond, 1945, p. 18.

Romans, your city has been overcome by brute force, but your rights are neither lessened nor changed. By all you hold sacred, citizens, keep yourselves uncontaminated. Organise peaceful demonstrations … In the streets, in the theatres, in every place of meeting let the same cries be heard. Thousands cannot be imprisoned. Men cannot be compelled to degrade themselves.

Why do you think Mazzini now emphasised peaceful protest in Source H?

Revolutionary defeats

The Pope returned to Rome in the afternoon of 12 April 1850 and was cheered through the streets by the same citizens who had cheered for Mazzini, Garibaldi and the Roman Republic a year earlier, evidence perhaps that even the return of the Pope was preferable to the hardships they had endured over the past months under French military occupation. Yet with the Pope also came the return of the repressive apparatus of papal rule: the Inquisition, corruption, public floggings and the guillotine.

Failure elsewhere

The Venetian Republic

The Roman Republic was not alone. There was another, the Venetian Republic, which had held out courageously against a siege by the Austrian navy, in the course of which the city was heavily shelled in the early summer of 1849. A severe outbreak of cholera added to the misery of starving Venetians, who were driven by their hunger and disease to surrender to the Austrians in August 1849. Manin was then forced into exile.

Piedmont

Earlier in the year Charles Albert, having apparently recovered from the horrors of his defeat at Custoza and his distress at abandoning Lombardy to the Austrians, decided in March to re-enter the war. (See pages 52–7 for more details of Charles Albert's rule in Piedmont.) Exactly why he made this decision is not clear. Some historians believe that he wanted revenge for his earlier defeat, others think that it was because he had had time to regroup his forces and was ready for action. He may also have believed, wrongly, that France would come to his aid if he re-entered the war.

Charles Albert was not to get his revenge. Within a month he was heavily defeated at the battle of Novara. This was the last straw. A broken man, he abdicated in favour of his son, Victor Emmanuel II.

Tuscany

In neighbouring Tuscany the Grand Duke had granted a constitution at the beginning of 1848. When news of the revolution in Vienna and the dismissal of Metternich reached Tuscany, the government decided to send a small army to fight the Austrians. Workers in the cities began to agitate about pay and conditions and middle-class radical extremists began to preach republicanism. In January 1849 the Grand Duke could stand it no longer and left for Naples, which still possessed an absolute monarchy. In Tuscany a revolutionary provisional government was set up and a **dictator** was appointed in advance of arrangements being made to proclaim a republic. Before this could be done, however, Charles Albert had been defeated at Novara. This left the Austrian army free to sweep down into Tuscany, where they crushed the revolution and restored the Grand Duke to his throne.

Much the same happened in Modena and Parma, where the rulers who fled to escape the revolutions were also restored to their thrones by Austrian military might.

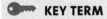

KEY TERM

Dictator Originally a term used in Ancient Rome to denote a chief magistrate with absolute power, appointed in an emergency.

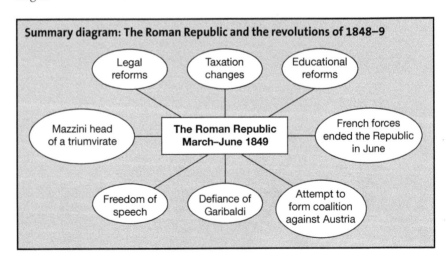

Summary diagram: The Roman Republic and the revolutions of 1848–9

- Legal reforms
- Taxation changes
- Educational reforms
- Mazzini head of a triumvirate
- **The Roman Republic March–June 1849**
- French forces ended the Republic in June
- Freedom of speech
- Defiance of Garibaldi
- Attempt to form coalition against Austria

Why did the revolutions fail?

▶ *What were the key factors in the failure of Italian nationalism?*

By the middle of 1849 it was clear that the revolutions it Italy had failed, just as they had in 1820 and 1831:

- In Sicily Neapolitan rule had been re-established and the Two Sicilies had been forcibly reunited under an even more absolute and repressive government than before.
- In the Papal States the Roman Republic had been destroyed and the Pope restored to his temporal power by the French soldiers who continued to occupy Rome. All expectations that Pius IX would be a liberal supporter of national unity for Italy were shattered.
- Tuscany, Modena and Parma found themselves again under absolute rule.
- The Venetian Republic came under tighter Austrian control, as did Lombardy.
- Worst of all, the strongest state, Piedmont, had suffered humiliating defeat by the Austrians in two battles. The only success for the revolutionaries was that the constitution, the *Statuto* (see page 54), granted to Piedmont by Charles Albert, survived and would continue to do so, eventually becoming the basis of the constitution of the new united Kingdom of Italy in 1860. But none of the other constitutions wrung from their rulers by the revolutionaries survived.
- None of the rulers forced to escape from their states was away for long.
- None of the states that gained independence – Sicily, Lombardy and Venetia – was able to retain it.

The revolutions had been an almost total failure, and a failure which had involved suffering and death for a very large number of people. As in the earlier revolutions, 'Italy' suffered from major drawbacks: a lack of unity, a lack of popular support and a lack of international allies.

Lack of unity

There was a lack of co-operation between the revolutionary groups. Those in Sicily and Naples were particularly at loggerheads. In Piedmont, Charles Albert would not accept volunteers from other states in his army, or work with any other revolutionary groups, unless they first declared their loyalty to the Piedmontese royal family.

The revolutionaries themselves were divided in their aims. Liberals believed that the granting of a constitution by the ruler was the necessary first step everywhere, but the radicals favoured republics. Both groups wanted to expel the foreign occupying power, Austria, but they could agree on little else.

There was no universally acceptable national leader who could co-ordinate policy. Of the three possible candidates, Mazzini, Pope Pius IX and Charles

Albert, none was acceptable to everyone. Local revolutionary leaders had no central guidance and the provisional governments that they set up could be any of the following: moderate, extremist, liberal, radical, republican, democratic or monarchist.

Lack of popular support

In the end it was not just that provisional governments and revolutionary movements lacked guidance in 1848–9. They were inexperienced, weak and lacking in resources, particularly military ones. They could not maintain themselves in power having gained it, partly owing to lack of support from the mass of the population, except perhaps while fighting was actually going on. The liberals did not in any case wish to encourage popular support or to involve the peasants. Politics, for them, was an elitist, middle-class affair. With few exceptions, peasants found themselves no better off under a liberal-dominated revolutionary government than they had been before. Social reform was not important to liberals and life did not improve for ordinary people.

Lack of international allies

The other vital explanation of revolutionary failure was the military power of Italy's enemies. Austria's military supremacy was probably the single most important factor in the failure of the revolutions. The Austrian armies were superior in numbers, better equipped and much better led than any other army in the peninsula. In any conflict they were bound to win, even if the revolutionary forces had been able to present a united front – which they did not. It was the Austrians who took the leading role in restoring the old regimes in 1849.

In 1848–9 Italian revolutionaries clearly needed allies to counter-balance the might of Austria. One major power (Austria) could only be defeated with the help of another. But the Pope's influence on the Catholic powers of Europe was clearly **counter-revolutionary**. France, Austria's traditional enemy, might have seemed at one stage a possible ally, but in fact France's only military action – crushing the Roman Republic – was ranged against Italian nationalists. In such a situation, there seemed very little cause for optimism in the nationalist camps.

A new dawn?

Italian nationalism suffered heavy blows with the defeat of the 1848 revolutions, but it was far from extinguished. Emotionally, 1848 reinforced nationalism. Many Italians felt revulsion at the brutal tactics the Austrian army had used and wished in particular to revenge Novara. Many Italians also drew strength from the memories and myths of the revolutions – from the Roman Republic and especially from the dramatic, against-the-odds defence of Garibaldi. His forced march with 5000 men from Rome to the Adriatic coast, along 800 kilometres of mountainous territory, with little food or water and pursued by the enemy,

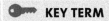

KEY TERM

Counter-revolutionary
Bringing about a revolution that is opposed to or reverses a former revolution.

became one of the glorious tales of the *Risorgimento*. Furthermore, the Italian situation was unexpectedly about to change in the 1850s. In Piedmont the *Statuto* remained in force and gave opportunities for political life to continue in ways that were not possible elsewhere in Italy. Refugees from other states came to Piedmont and settled there, more than 200,000 in Turin and Genoa. They gave Piedmont a cosmopolitan air and a more nationalist flavour which paved the way for what was to come in the person of Count Camillo Benso di Cavour. He was to be one of the great figures in the history of the unification of Italy. But for Italian nationalism to succeed there also had to be changes in European politics, and in particular the emergence of a powerful ally.

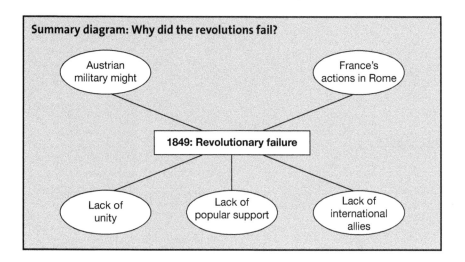

Summary diagram: Why did the revolutions fail?

Chapter summary

The restoration of the pre-Napoleonic regimes to Italy in 1815 failed to meet the aspirations of growing numbers of middle-class Italians. Liberals, radicals and increasing numbers of nationalists wanted significant political change. Resistance to their demands produced three sets of revolutions, in 1820–2, 1831–2 and 1848–9, all of which were defeated. These failures were due to the weakness of the revolutionaries, in that they lacked both unity and mass support as well as outside help, and to the strength not so much of the existing regimes as of the Austrian state that dominated them. The Italian rebels were no military match for the might of the Austrian army, as demonstrated in the battles of Custoza (in July 1848) and Novara (March 1849).

Nevertheless, undoubted progress was made by Italian nationalists over the 1815–49 period: 'Young Italy', founded in 1831, was much closer to a real political party than the *Carbonari* and other secret societies had been, and Mazzini was a dedicated revolutionary of considerable talent. Defeat in 1848–9 did not extinguish Italian nationalism and valuable lessons were learned, in particular that outside help was needed to overcome Austrian domination.

Refresher questions

Use these questions to remind yourself of the key material covered in this chapter.

1 Why were there so many groups of Italians after 1815 dissatisfied with the political *status quo*?

2 How important were the *Carbonari*?

3 Why did the revolutions of 1820–1 fail?

4 How close did the revolutions of 1831–2 come to success?

5 How realistic were Mazzini's ideas?

6 How important was Mazzini as an Italian nationalist?

7 In what ways was 'Young Italy' an effective political force?

8 What role did Pope Pius IX play in the 1848 revolutions?

9 Why did the revolutions of 1848 enjoy early success in Italy?

10 Did the Roman Republic of 1849 achieve anything of note?

11 Why did the nationalists fail to elicit mass support?

12 Why was the international situation unfavourable for Italian nationalism before 1850?

13 In what ways did the situation change after 1850?

 Question practice

ESSAY QUESTIONS

1 'The revolutions of 1820–1 and 1831–2 failed largely because of divisions and weaknesses among the revolutionaries.' How far do you agree?

2 'Mazzini's Roman Republic was the greatest success of the revolutions of 1848–9 in Italy.' How far do you agree with this view?

3 How accurate is it to say that very little progress was made in unifying Italians in the period from 1820 to 1848?

4 How far do you agree that the weaknesses and divisions of the nationalists were the principal reason for the failure of the 1848 revolutions in Italy?

INTERPRETATION QUESTION

1 Read the interpretation then answer the question that follows: 'The lesson of the 1848–9 revolutions was that Austria held the key to Italian unity and had no intention of unlocking the door.' (From *The Unification of Italy*, A. Stiles, 2006, p. 28.) Evaluate the strengths and limitations of this interpretation, making reference to other interpretations that you have studied.

SOURCE ANALYSIS QUESTIONS

1 Why is Source 1 valuable to the historian for an enquiry into the early success of the 1848 revolutions in northern Italy? Explain your answer using the source, the information about it and your own knowledge of the historical context.

2 How much weight do you give the evidence of Source 2 for an enquiry into the social improvements brought about by Mazzini's Roman Republic? Explain your answer using the source, the information about it and your own knowledge of the historical context.

3 How far could the historian make use of Sources 3 and 4 (page 48) to investigate the initial successes of the 1848 revolutions in Italy? Explain your answer using the sources, the information you have about them and your own knowledge of the historical context.

SOURCE 1

Dispatches from Field Marshal Radetsky, the 81-year-old commander of the Austrian army in Italy, to the Austrian minister in Vienna, 18–22 March 1848, quoted in Denis Mack Smith, *The Making of Italy, 1796–1866*, Palgrave Macmillan, 1988, pp. 141–5.

March 18–19: I am determined to remain master of Milan whatever happens. I shall bombard the city … March 21: The revolutionary party is moving with a caution and cleverness which make it obvious that they are being directed from abroad … My information from the provinces, though slight, is very alarming, for the whole country is in revolt and even the peasants are armed … At nine o'clock the news spread that the Piedmontese army had deployed along the Ticino and that groups of volunteers had already crossed the river … March 22: It is the most frightful decision of my life, but I can no longer hold Milan. The whole country is in revolt. I am pressed in the rear by the Piedmontese … I shall withdraw towards Lodi to avoid the large towns and while the countryside is still open.

SOURCE 2

Decrees issued by the Roman Republic, April 1849, quoted in F. Eyck, editor, *The Revolutions of 1848–49*, Oliver & Boyd, 1972, pp. 138–9.

Whereas it is the office and duty of a well-organised Republic to provide for the gradual amelioration of the condition of the most necessitous classes:

Whereas the improvement most urgent at the present moment is that of withdrawing as many families as possible from the evils resulting from crowded and unhealthy habitations … the Constituent Assembly, at the suggestion of the Triumvirs, degrees:

(1) The edifice hitherto used as the Holy Office is henceforth dedicated to the use of necessitous families or individuals, who shall be allowed to have lodgings therein on payment of a small monthly rent …

(2) A large portion of the rural domains belonging to religious corporations … shall be immediately divided into a given number of portions sufficient for the maintenance of one or more necessitous families having no other means of support …

SOURCE 3

From notices posted up in Palermo, quoted in Giorgio Candeloro, *Stori deli' Italia moderna*, second edition, volume III, Feltrinelli, 1966, p. 122.

Sicilians! the time for prayers is past; peaceful protests and demonstrations have all been useless. Ferdinand, King of Naples, has treated them all with contempt and we, as people born free, are loaded with chains and reduced to misery. Shall we still delay claiming our lawful rights? To arms, sons of Sicily; our united force will be invincible …

SOURCE 4

From an appeal by the provisional government of Milan to its fellow citizens, March 1848, quoted in Frank Eyck, *The Revolutions of 1848–49*, Barnes & Noble Books, 1972, p. 72.

We have conquered. We have compelled the enemy to fly, oppressed as much by his own shame as our valour; but scattered in our fields, wandering like wild beasts, united in bands of plunderers, he prolonged for us the horrors of war without affording any of its sublime emotions. This makes it easy to understand that the arms we have taken up, and still hold, can never be laid down as long as one of his band shall be hid under cover of the Alps. We have sworn, we swear it again, with the generous Prince who flies to associate himself with our glory – all Italy swears it and so it shall be.

To arms then, to arms, to secure the fruits of our glorious revolution – to fight the last battle of independence and the Italian Union.

CHAPTER 3

Piedmont, Cavour and Italy

This chapter considers the way in which the northern state of Piedmont spearheaded the successful unification of Italy under its prime minister, Count Camillo di Cavour. The main areas to consider are:

★ Piedmont and Charles Albert

★ Cavour

★ The role of Napoleon III

★ The war of 1859

★ Cavour and Garibaldi

Try to avoid making any final judgements on Garibaldi until you have read Chapter 4.

Key dates

1815		Victor Emmanuel I returned to Piedmont as one of the Restored Monarchs
1821		Victor Emmanuel I abdicated
1831		Charles Albert became King of Piedmont
1848	Feb.	Charles Albert issued the *Statuto*
	March 23	Charles Albert declared war on Austria
	July	Charles Albert defeated at Custoza
1849	March	Charles Albert defeated at Novara
		Charles Albert abdicated; succeeded by Victor Emmanuel II
1852		Cavour became prime minister

1855–6		Piedmont participated in the Crimean War
1858	July	Cavour and Louis Napoleon met at Plombières
1859	April 29	France and Piedmont went to war with Austria
	June 4	The battle of Magenta
	June 24	The battle of Solferino
	July 11	Truce at Villafranca
	July	Cavour resigned
1860	Jan.	Cavour resumed the premiership of Piedmont
		Garibaldi's conquest of southern Italy
1861	March	Victor Emmanuel proclaimed King of Italy
		Death of Cavour

Piedmont and Charles Albert

▶ *Why did Piedmont become so central to the unification process?*
▶ *How significant a role did Charles Albert play in Italian unification?*

In 1720 the Dukes of Savoy, who ruled over the then poor and backward state of Piedmont in north-west Italy, became kings of the island of Sardinia. Piedmont and Sardinia together came to be known as the Kingdom of Sardinia, or Sardinia-Piedmont, but most usually just as Piedmont.

At the end of the eighteenth century Piedmont had only a small population, most of whom were peasants. Although a large number of children were born, the death rate was very high and life expectancy was short. The number of people living in the capital, Turin, was declining, there was little or no industry, and the countryside was poverty stricken. Nevertheless, Piedmont had two advantages over neighbouring states:

- Unlike the other states it had a strong army.
- It was efficiently governed by an absolute monarch. The king, as head of state, made all the decisions and all the laws, decided what taxes should be levied and what they should be spent on, and appointed government ministers. He alone could declare war or make peace. There was no parliament and so the people had no share in government, no votes and no say in what happened.

French rule

At the end of the eighteenth century Piedmont made an alliance with Austria. The Piedmontese royal family was closely connected by marriage with the French royal family and this made them automatically an enemy of the French Republic, which had deposed and executed Louis XVI, and then of Napoleon. In 1792, when the French army attacked Nice and Savoy, to the west of Piedmont, Austria and Piedmont declared war on France.

The war went badly for the allies with the result that, during 1799 and again from 1802 to 1814, Piedmont was united with France. This meant that Piedmont came into very close contact with French law and French government organisation:

- Piedmontese schools became part of the French education system.
- Piedmont's young men were conscripted into the French army.
- French became the language of polite society as well as of government, and the well-to-do members of society became more and more French in outlook.

There was no great opposition to French rule and the middle classes even found it to their advantage as it provided career opportunities. They were allowed to fill posts in government service and in the army that had previously been reserved only for members of the nobility. Only towards the end of French occupation was there unrest and dissatisfaction, with young men setting up anti-French secret societies.

A period of reaction 1815–31

In 1815 the King of Piedmont, Victor Emmanuel I, who had been in exile in Sardinia during the Napoleonic years, returned to Turin as one of the Restored Monarchs (see page 8). To make himself more welcome he abolished conscription and reduced taxation; but on his ministers' advice he announced that Piedmont was still bound by the laws made before 1800, which many considered out of date, and that these could not be changed. Piedmont became once again an absolute monarchy. The French legal system, the *Code Napoléon* (see page 6), was abolished along with equal justice for all. Criminal trials were no longer open or fair, although at least torture was not reintroduced.

There seemed little hope of progressive reforms, especially since, in 1819, there were alarms about the possibility of a revolution. Moderate Piedmontese pinned their hopes not on Victor Emmanuel I or his brother and heir **Charles Felix** but on the second in line to the throne, Charles Albert.

On his return to Piedmont in 1815 from exile in France, where he had lived since his father had died when he was only two years old, Charles Albert saw just how severe and oppressive Piedmont's government had become. He showed sympathy with revolutionary students injured in riots in Turin and was known to have connections with revolutionary officers in the army. In March 1821 the liberals appealed to him to lead a revolution. Initially he agreed, but soon he changed his mind.

While Charles Albert was dithering, a revolutionary group had seized the fortress of Alessandria in Genoa and established a provisional government calling itself the 'Kingdom of Italy' and, rather foolishly, declaring war on Austria.

Abdication

At this stage the 62-year-old Victor Emmanuel, tired of being pressured by revolutionary groups to grant political and social reforms and worried by reports of new army mutinies in Turin, decided to abdicate. He left for Nice, close to the western frontier of Piedmont, as revolution spread throughout his kingdom.

Victor Emmanuel's heir, and younger brother, Charles Felix, was away from Piedmont and so Charles Albert seized the initiative and set up a new government and granted a new constitution. But when Charles Felix denounced him as a usurper, Charles Albert fled and the legitimate monarch gained control of Piedmont with the aid of Austrian forces. He promptly revoked the new constitution. Only in 1831, when Charles Felix died, did Charles Albert become, at last, King of Piedmont.

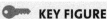

KEY FIGURE

Charles Felix (1765–1831)

King of Piedmont from 1821 to 1831. His undistinguished reign was marked by political repression and economic stagnation.

Charles Albert

Politics

The new king's earlier career had been marked by contradictions, and the same pattern now reasserted itself, so that it is very difficult for historians to interpret his real aims.

On the one hand, Charles Albert could give the impression of being an old-fashioned ruler, as in the illustration in Source A. It seemed that he would be as absolute and oppressive a monarch as Victor Emmanuel or Charles Felix:

- He began his reign by signing a treaty with Austria and threatening to attack the liberal government then in power in France.
- He refused to pardon the political prisoners left over from the 1821 revolutions.
- He increased the power of the Church in Piedmont.
- He tightened the already severe censorship laws.

Small wonder, then, that Mazzini and Garibaldi, two key nationalist figures, left Piedmont, soon to be followed by Gioberti (see page 32) who, anxious to publish his proposals for a federation of Italian states presided over by the Pope, left for the liberal city of Brussels. Another figure, Count Camillo di Cavour, also left Piedmont, which he dubbed 'that intellectual hell', preferring the greater freedom of expression found almost anywhere else, even in Austrian Lombardy.

On the other hand, some of Charles Albert's actions were those of a reformer:

- He made helpful changes in trade laws, reducing duties on imported goods and signing trade treaties with other states.
- He tidied up the legal system and its laws.
- He allowed non-nobles to fill senior posts in the army and the royal advisory council.
- Most important of all, in 1848–9 he granted his people a constitution that would survive to become the constitution of the united Italy of the 1860s.

Motives and character

Historians have tried to explain why Charles Albert changed from a liberal to reactionary and back to being a liberal again, but have not found any satisfactory answer. Truly he was, as some contemporaries dubbed him, *Re Tentenua* – 'the wobbling king'.

One suggestion is that he had always been a nationalist, perhaps even a secret revolutionary; and, once king, was only waiting for a suitable opportunity to declare himself. *'Italia fara da se'* ('Italy will make herself by herself'), he famously insisted in the 1840s. Perhaps this was his wish all along. Yet this interpretation is not very convincing, since several of his actions after 1831, for instance his alliance with Austria, were reactionary.

SOURCE A

A portrait of Charles Albert on horseback, *c*.1885.

What aspects of Source A make the king seem a traditional ruler of the *ancien régime*?

Part of the answer must lie in Charles Albert's own complicated character. Many described him as secretive and unsociable, seldom showing any emotion, and some have believed him out of touch with reality. His attraction to the more mystical aspects of Catholicism, and his habit of wearing a **hair shirt**, are not necessarily signs of mental imbalance. But his belief that he was cut out to be a soldier and a leader of men was at best unrealistic. Admittedly, he could be energetic and enterprising on occasions, but he lacked sustained determination as well as high-level abilities. Yet Charles Albert took to heart the idea of himself as a military leader and even came to believe, with disastrous results, that he was the military genius who would destroy the Austrian hold on Lombardy and Venetia.

 **KEY TERM**

Hair shirt A garment made of haircloth, causing discomfort to the body and thereby, according to believers, bringing its wearer closer to God.

Changing times

To understand fully Charles Albert's actions we also need to be aware of the changing circumstances in which his policies were made. Liberal influences were growing, so that from 1841, for instance, non-political gatherings, such as scientific conferences, were allowed for the first time. Although seemingly non-political, such meetings often helped to spread liberal and nationalist ideas. At one such congress, held in 1846, Charles Albert was referred to as 'the Italian leader who would drive out the foreigners', an idea that appealed to the king's vanity and gave him immense satisfaction.

As the 1840s wore on, the pressure for liberal reforms grew. In Turin there were peaceful demands for a constitution from the small but well-educated and outspoken middle and professional social classes. In Genoa, still smarting from the loss of its independence (see page 9) and where Mazzini was a major influence, demands were more violent and revolutionary.

1848 and the *Statuto*

The unrest in Turin spread, culminating in October 1847 in noisy demonstrations and threats of revolution that persuaded Charles Albert to agree to reforms and to grant a constitution early in the following year. As a devout Catholic he was probably also influenced by the limited reforms recently introduced in the Papal States by Pius IX in his liberal phase (see page 33).

Charles Albert's general reforms were aimed at taking some of the power away from the monarchy and putting it into the hands of government officials. For instance, the police were in future to be under the control of the **minister of the interior**. Local government was also reorganised and local councils were elected.

The constitution that the king had promised was issued in the form of fourteen articles on 8 February 1848 and was known as the *Statuto* (see Source B, opposite).

The stress on representative government here must have cheered the reformers, but the articles were not very clearly expressed. Perhaps this was intentional, as a means by which Charles Albert might avoid giving away too much of his power. Phrases such as 'The king's ministers are responsible' left it uncertain for what or to whom they were responsible – to the king? To the chambers? To the people? Equally unclear is the reference to the 'restraining laws' limiting the freedom of the press. Some form of censorship is implied, but we do not know how moderate or severe it might be.

The full *Statuto* was published in March 1848 and included a number of other clauses relating to legal equality for all, whatever their religion, and for equal employment opportunities. It did not lay down who would elect members of the lower chamber. This was fixed later when the vote was given to men who could read and write and who paid taxes – in fact only about two per cent of the population of Piedmont.

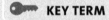

KEY TERM

Minister of the interior
The European equivalent of the British home secretary, the minister responsible for, among other things, police and internal security.

SOURCE B

From the *Statuto*, quoted in Gran Bretagna, Part II, *Correspondence Respecting the Affairs of Italy, From January to June 30, 1848, Presented to Both Houses of Parliament by Command of Her Majesty, July 1849*, Harrison & Son, 1849, p. 68.

A constitution is announced:

Now, therefore, that the times are ripe for greater things and, in the midst of the changes which have occurred in Italy, we hesitate no longer to give our people the most solemn proof that we are able to give of the faith which we continue to repose in their devotion and discretion …

We have resolved and determined to adopt the following bases of a fundamental statute for the establishment in our states of a complete system of representative Government …

Article 2 The person of the Sovereign is sacred and inviolable. His ministers are responsible.

Article 3 To the King alone belongs the executive power. He is the supreme head of the State. He commands all the forces both naval and military; declares war, concludes treaties of peace, alliance and commerce; nominates to all offices, and gives all the necessary orders for the execution of the laws without suspending or dispensing with the observance thereof …

Article 6 The legislative power will be collectively exercised by the King and the two Chambers.

Article 7 The first of these Chambers will be composed of members nominated by the King for life; the second will be elective, on the basis of the census to be determined.

Article 8 The proposal of laws will appertain to the King and to each of the Chambers but with the distinct understanding that all laws imposing taxes must originate in the elective Chamber …

Article 10 No tax may be imposed or levied if not assented to by the Chambers and sanctioned by the King.

Article 11 The press will be free but subject to restraining laws.

Article 12 Individual liberty will be guaranteed.

> To what extent did the *Statuto* shown in Source B change the politics of Piedmont?

The constitution was not a parliamentary one except in a very limited way, since it allowed the king to keep most of his existing rights. Nevertheless, it was undoubtedly a major advance. Many of Charles Albert's ministers thought it too extreme and so resigned, being replaced by more liberal-minded men.

Piedmont and Italian unification

Meanwhile, events outside Piedmont were moving rapidly and may well have influenced Charles Albert's decision to proclaim the constitution. Revolutions in Sicily, Naples, Lombardy and Venetia broke out in rapid succession between

January and March 1848 (see pages 34–6). In Austrian Lombardy, Piedmont's eastern neighbour, extreme revolutionaries wanted an independent republic, while more moderate ones wanted union with Piedmont. Charles Albert saw advantages in putting himself at the head of a Lombard revolt against Austria, as eventually Piedmont might be able to dominate or even annex Lombardy. Typically, he hesitated, however, undecided whether to take military action or not, afraid that his absence might allow his own revolutionaries to stir up trouble in Genoa, the part of Piedmont most likely to organise a revolution.

War with Austria

Eventually, public pressure and news that the revolutionary government now established in Venetia had voted for union with Piedmont persuaded Charles Albert to declare war on 23 March 1848: 'For the purpose of more fully showing by outward signs the sentiments of Italian unity, we wish that our troops should enter the territory of Lombardy and Venetia, bearing the arms of Savoy [the royal family of Piedmont] above the Italian tri-coloured flag'.

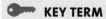

KEY TERM

Imperialistic Motivated by the desire to dominate or capture other people's territory.

Again, historians have argued about Charles Albert's motives. Did he act out of self-interest in the expectation of Lombardy and Venetia being 'fused' with Piedmont as the price of his help, thus merely clothing essentially **imperialistic** aims with appropriately nationalistic language? Or was he genuinely concerned to support a revolt against the foreigner, Austria, and make himself leader of a national independence movement?

The decision to act finally made, Charles Albert entered the war with enthusiasm. His army of 60,000 men, incompetently led by himself and ill-prepared for war, crossed into Lombardy and occupied the capital, Milan. The Austrians, who had already evacuated the city, brought up reinforcements and defeated Charles Albert at Custoza on the border with Venetia. The king had no choice but to ask for an armistice. This allowed the Piedmontese army to withdraw from Lombardy, leaving it again in Austrian hands.

Charles Albert broke the news to his people in a carefully edited version of events, insisting that 'want of provisions forced us to abandon the positions we had conquered. ... Even the strength of brave soldiers has its limits'. He added that his people should now 'show themselves strong in misfortune' and have confidence in their king, for the 'cause of Italian independence is not yet lost'.

Early in 1849, having regrouped his forces and been persuaded, incorrectly, by his chief minister that Louis Napoleon, the newly elected president of the French Republic, would come to his aid if Piedmont again attacked Austria, Charles Albert re-entered the war but with even less success than before. Piedmontese forces, under the command of an experienced but ailing Polish general, Wojciech Chrzanowski, were no match for the experienced troops of General Radetsky. Charles Albert was heavily defeated by the Austrians at Novara, and then abdicated in favour of his son.

Charles Albert's legacy

The king's unsuccessful attempt to defeat Austria in battle was a major blow for Italian nationalists. Clearly, while Austria remained so powerful there was no way in which Italy could gain independence or unity without outside help. Yet at least this blunt fact was now obvious, and future Italian leaders could learn this lesson. Almost no one now subscribed to Charles Albert's earlier notion that '*Italia farà da sé*'.

Charles Albert's other main legacy was the *Statuto*, which outlived him, the one tangible result in Italy of the revolutions of 1848. **Victor Emmanuel II**, who succeeded his father in March 1849, has traditionally been seen as a courageous figure defying Austrian plans for the *Statuto*'s abolition. Yet most historians now think that Victor Emmanuel was not particularly anxious to keep the constitution but was pressured into doing so by the Austrians themselves, who feared that if he got rid of it he would become so unpopular that not only he, but the monarchy itself, would be threatened. In Austrian eyes anything, even a state with a moderately liberal constitution, was better than a republic.

The constitution therefore remained in force, and in spite of its limitations gave an opportunity for an active political life in Piedmont, something that did not then exist anywhere else in Italy. With a reasonably free press, an elected if unrepresentative assembly, and a certain amount of civil liberty and legal equality, Piedmont attracted refugees from the rest of Italy during the next decade. This was to be a period dominated by the political leadership of Cavour, the military successes of Garibaldi and the interventions of Louis Napoleon of France.

🔑 **KEY FIGURE**

Victor Emmanuel II (1820–78)

King of Piedmont 1849–61 and then King of a united Italy 1861–78. He appointed Cavour as prime minister in 1852 and pressed him to join the Crimean War two years later. Hailed in Italy as the 'Father of the Fatherland' (*Padre della Patria*), his primary loyalty was focused on Piedmont-Sardinia.

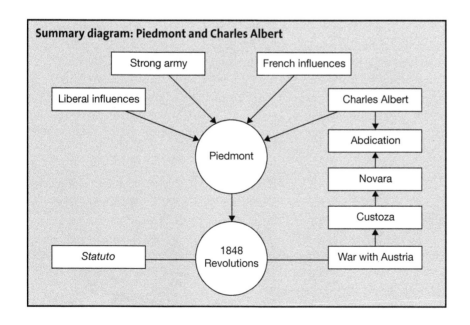

Summary diagram: Piedmont and Charles Albert

Cavour

▶ *How important was Cavour in the creation of a united and independent Italy?*

▶ *How successful was Cavour in domestic and foreign affairs?*

Cavour as prime minister

Cavour became prime minister in 1852. His previous experience had given him an expert knowledge of economic and financial affairs, and under his guidance Piedmont undoubtedly became a more developed and richer state. Its trade increased, its industries flourished and its railways become the envy of the rest of Italy. This economic development put the state in a strong position to dominate Italy politically.

> ### Piedmont's economic development in the 1850s
>
> - Imports and exports almost quadrupled.
> - Industries flourished.
> - Trade treaties were negotiated with Britain, France, Austria, Portugal and Belgium.
> - By 1859 Piedmont had 850 kilometres of railway track, almost as much as the rest of Italy put together (with 980 kilometres).

Yet in 1852 Cavour had only a limited knowledge and understanding of foreign affairs. In the 1830s he had expressed a vague wish that Italy should be united and free from Austrian domination. He hoped, he said, 'for the soonest possible emancipation of Italy from the barbarians who oppress her' but was worried because 'a crisis of at least some violence is inevitable'. He wanted this crisis 'to be as restrained as the state of things allows' because he feared that revolutionary movements, with their stress on republicanism and social upheaval, 'would only make unity more difficult to achieve'. But too much should not be read into these remarks, for in the 1850s he still referred on a number of occasions to the idea of Italian unity as 'rubbish'. Probably he did not begin to see it as a realistic aim until 1859.

The Crimean War

Cavour quickly gained experience in foreign affairs. Two years after he took office an international crisis led to the start of the **Crimean War**. Traditionally, Cavour has been seen as happily joining in the war against Russia in order to gain the friendship of Britain and France and to be sure of some of the spoils, as well as a seat at the eventual peace conference. Undoubtedly, this motive did influence his decision to join in the war.

 **KEY TERM**

Crimean War A war fought in 1854–6 by Britain and France, with some support from Piedmont, against Russia. Austria decided to remain neutral.

Camillo Benso di Cavour

1811	Born in Piedmont, the second son of a rich noble, who was a successful businessman and politician
1821	Sent away to the Royal Military Academy
1820s	Worked for a short time in the service of Charles Albert, and then became an officer in the army. Developed an interest in economics and politics
1833	Left the army and visited London and Paris, his interest sparked by Britain's industrial and financial success
1835	Returned to Piedmont. Took over family estate, importing artificial fertilisers and making use of new agricultural methods and machinery
1846	Wrote on his favourite subject, railways, which he described as the great marvel of the nineteenth century. Helped to set up the Bank of Turin, himself becoming one of its first ten directors
1847	Charles Albert freed the press from censorship and Cavour founded his own publication, *Il Risorgimento*. Elected to the first Piedmontese parliament; became well known as a liberal politician
1850	Appointed minister of agriculture, commerce and the navy. Negotiated free trade treaties. Prime Minister Massimo d'Azeglio did not enjoy the everyday business of government

and handed over much of it to Cavour

1851	Became minister of finance
1852	Fell out of sympathy with d'Azeglio's traditionally minded government, and made an alliance with a moderately radical party in parliament to form a new centre party. Encouraged to do this by d'Azeglio's decision to reduce the freedom of the press slightly
	Resigned as a minister in May. Went abroad, and met the president of the French Republic, Louis Napoleon
	Asked by Victor Emmanuel II in November to form a government on condition he dropped d'Azeglio's controversial **civil marriage** bill, which aroused the opposition of the papacy. Cavour was himself a **secularist**, but reluctantly accepted. He remained as prime minister, apart from a few months in 1859–60, until his early death
1861	Died

The nine years of Cavour's premiership were some of the most momentous in the history of Italy. By the time of his death, all of Italy apart from Venetia and Rome had been unified. Controversy centres on how important his role was in this process, and on whether he actually intended that the Italian peninsula, rather than merely northern Italy, should be unified.

Cavour's speech to parliament in 1855 presented his vision of a new Italy whose international reputation would be improved further by sending young men to fight in the war, rather than staying at home and taking part in revolutions, plots and conspiracies which damaged Italy's reputation abroad (see Source C).

Nevertheless, there is evidence that Cavour was doubtful. He was swayed by the king, who was eager to take part in the conflict, and also by Britain and France. These countries put pressure on Cavour partly because they knew that additional, Piedmontese, troops would be useful in the conflict and partly because of a more subtle motive. They wanted Austria, as well as Piedmont, to join the war and they reasoned that, if both these states were on the same side, the Austrians would be reassured that Piedmont would not interfere in Lombardy.

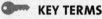 **KEY TERMS**

Civil marriage Marriage without a church service.

Secularist One who favours the state over the Church.

? How far does the speech in Source C help to explain why Cavour decided to intervene in the Crimean War?

SOURCE C

From Cavour's speech to parliament in 1855, quoted in Edward Henry Nolan, *The Liberators of Italy: Or, the Lives of Garibaldi; Victor Emmanuel, King of Italy; Count Cavour; and Napoleon III, Emperor of the French*, James S. Virtue, 1864, p. 274.

The sons of Italy can fight with true valour on the field of glory … I am sure that the laurels our soldiers will win on the battlefields of the east will do more for the future of Italy than all those who have thought to revive her with the voice and with the pen … so that she can take her rightful place among the Great Powers.

Either way, by joining in the war Cavour did achieve his aim of a seat at the peace conference held in Paris in 1856. There he was able to negotiate on almost equal terms with the Great Powers, and there he also made the further acquaintance of Louis Napoleon, now Emperor Napoleon III. They kept in touch over the next two years until, in July 1858, Cavour was invited to a meeting at Plombières, close to the Franco-Swiss border.

The Plombières meeting

This meeting was kept very secret – even the French foreign minister was not aware of what was happening. Cavour was equally secretive. He had told only Victor Emmanuel and one other minister about the meeting, which was beginning to look like a conspiracy.

Whose were the proposals discussed at Plombières? Napoleon had issued the invitation and organised the meeting. It might be expected that the meeting's agenda would be his, but there is evidence to suggest that Cavour took with him an outline memorandum that contained proposals very similar to what was finally agreed.

Three days later, on 24 July, Cavour sat down and wrote a very long and detailed letter to Victor Emmanuel giving his version of the discussion (see Source D).

? According to Source D, how determined was the French emperor on a war with Austria?

SOURCE D

From a letter written to Victor Emmanuel in July 1858, quoted in Denis Mack Smith, *The Making of Italy*, Palgrave Macmillan, 1988, pp. 238–47.

As soon as I entered the Emperor's study, he raised the question which was the purpose of my journey. He began by saying that he had decided to support Piedmont with all his power in a war against Austria, provided that the war was undertaken for a non-revolutionary end which could be justified in the eyes of diplomatic circles, and still more in the eyes of French and European public opinion.

Both men were aware that unless the war seemed reasonable to Europe's leaders, Austria might find allies. Certainly, Prussia made it clear that it might support its German neighbour, Austria; and even Britain, though generally sympathetic to Italian aspirations, would not support a war of unprovoked aggression.

Furthermore, the Great Powers were fearful that Austrian domination might well be replaced by French control. If this fear proved justified, there might have to be a coalition of Great Powers to defeat this new Napoleon.

Of course, the ideal solution, for Cavour and Napoleon III, would be if Austria could be manoeuvred into declaring war. But, failing this, what might be a suitable issue on which France and Piedmont could start the war?

'The search for a plausible excuse presented our main problem', Cavour told his king. He suggested that the Austrian emperor had broken certain commercial agreements and had extended his territory in Italy further than treaties allowed, but the emperor thought that such 'pretexts' would not justify war. The two men racked their brains to hit on a possible solution, but could not think of any.

Unable to find a suitable excuse for France and Piedmont to make war on Austria and drive it out of Italy, the two men focused instead on how a future Austria-free Italy would be organised:

- There would be a kingdom of Upper Italy, based on Piedmont and ruled over by the House of Savoy, the Piedmontese royal family.
- Rome and its immediately surrounding area would be left to the control of the Pope.
- The rest of the Papal States, together with Tuscany, would form a kingdom of Central Italy.
- Naples and Sicily would be untouched.
- These four Italian states would form a **confederation**, with its presidency going to the Pope, to console him for losing control of the bulk of the Papal States.

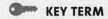

KEY TERM

Confederation A loose alliance of states.

Cavour told his king that this arrangement was fully acceptable: Victor Emmanuel would become 'the legal sovereign of the richest and most powerful half of Italy, and hence would in practice dominate the whole peninsula'.

Next, Louis Napoleon and Cavour considered what benefits France might receive from fighting a war against Austria (see Source E).

The outcome

A deal was almost struck:

- Napoleon estimated that an army of around 300,000 men would be needed to drive Austria out of Italy: he would provide 200,000 and Piedmont and other Italian states 100,000.
- Italy would become four states, loosely grouped under the Pope as a figurehead. (A united Italy, if one were possible, might become a threat to France or arouse the suspicions of the other Great Powers. For further consideration of Louis Napoleon's motives, see pages 65–7.) Piedmont's power would grow considerably.
- As a reward, France would receive Savoy. Whether Nice would also be handed over was at this stage uncertain.

The Unification of Italy 1789–1896

From Cavour's version of the Plombières agreement sent to Victor Emanuel, quoted in Derek Beales and Eugenio F. Biagini, *The Risorgimento and the Unification of Italy*, Routledge, 2014, p. 263.

The Emperor asked me whether Your Majesty would cede Savoy and the County of Nice. I answered that Your Majesty believed in the principle of nationalities and realised accordingly that Savoy ought to be reunited with France; and that consequently you were prepared to make this sacrifice, even though it would be extremely painful to renounce the country which had been the cradle of your family and whose people had given your ancestors so many proofs of affection and devotion. The question of Nice was different, because the people of Nice, by origin, language and customs were closer to Piedmont than to France.

What, according to Cavour in Source E, was the essential difference between transferring Savoy and transferring Nice to France?

- The diplomatic ground would have to be prepared carefully, so that Austria would have no allies. Hence, a good excuse for war would have to be found, although as yet neither Cavour nor Napoleon could devise one.
- A provisional agreement was also reached for a marriage between Victor Emmanuel's daughter, Clothilde, and one of Napoleon's cousins.

The arrangements reached at Plombières were largely incorporated into a secret treaty in January 1859, although some changes were made. In particular, Nice was added to Savoy as Napoleon's proposed reward, and the idea of an Italian confederation headed by the Pope was abandoned. But there was a major stumbling block that might prevent the war being fought: could a suitable pretext for war be devised?

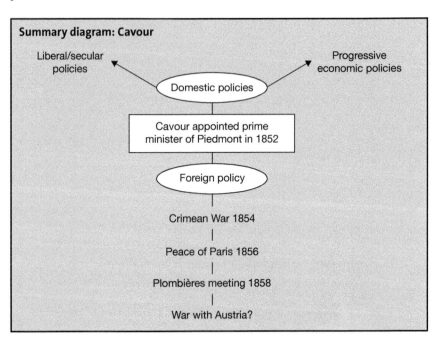

Summary diagram: Cavour

Liberal/secular policies ← Domestic policies → Progressive economic policies

Cavour appointed prime minister of Piedmont in 1852

Foreign policy

Crimean War 1854

Peace of Paris 1856

Plombières meeting 1858

War with Austria?

3 The role of Napoleon III

▶ *What was the probable mix of motives that influenced Napoleon's actions in Italy?*

▶ *Why did Napoleon destroy Mazzini's regime in Rome?*

Louis Napoleon: romantic adventurer

The nephew of Napoleon Bonaparte (the Emperor Napoleon I), Louis Napoleon had no intention of leading a 'normal' life. Conspiracy, adventure and the search for power and prestige seemed to be part of his heritage. He was in Italy during the winter of the revolutionary year 1830–1, attempting to capture the Pope's castle of Saint Angelo, to proclaim his cousin, the son of Napoleon I, as King of Italy. He was signally unsuccessful, but this episode was the beginning of Louis Napoleon's love affair with Italian nationalism. Although his actions were often unpredictable, and although there was an element of self-interest in almost all he did, it was to be with his aid, in the end, that Italian independence and unity were achieved.

Louis Napoleon Bonaparte

1808	Born in Paris, the third son of Louis Bonaparte, the brother of Napoleon I. Brought up in exile in Switzerland
1831	Expelled from Rome after attempted coup
1832	Became head of the Napoleonic dynasty
1836	Involved in a failed coup in Paris
1840	Involved in a second failed coup in Paris
1848	Elected president of the French Republic
1849	His forces destroyed the Roman Republic
1852	Became Emperor of France after a successful coup. At home, he encouraged economic expansion; abroad, he sought glory and prestige
1854–6	Involved in Crimean War. He was on the winning side against Russia
1859	Defeated Austria and furthered the cause of Italian independence
1860	Gained Nice and Savoy for France
1862–5	Intervention in Mexico ended in disaster
1870–1	Franco-Prussian War
1871	Went into exile in England, where he lived until his death
1873	Died

Controversy has always surrounded the career of Louis Napoleon, especially the issue of his motives, including why he supported the cause of Italian unification. The fact that he was a member of the Bonaparte family is crucial here. 'When a man of my name is in power', he insisted, 'he must do great things'. At least he had to *try* to do great things. Also hotly debated is the level of ability he possessed. The leader of Prussia, and then Germany, Otto von Bismarck, was certainly not impressed with him. After one meeting he wrote the following about Napoleon III: 'Far afar, something; near at hand, nothing: a great, unfathomed incapacity.'

Louis Napoleon and the Roman Republic

In the 1830s Louis Napoleon's wish to help the Italians seemed sincere, but in March 1849, when the Roman Republic was proclaimed with Mazzini at its head and Garibaldi as its military leader (see page 40), he reacted very differently, as a counter-revolutionary rather than a supporter of nationalism. He was now no longer a hopeful rebel, having been elected president of the French Republic a few months earlier.

Pius IX fled Rome during the revolutions of 1848 and took refuge in Naples. He appealed to the Catholic monarchs of Europe, but no help came. Yet Louis Napoleon was prepared to act. He knew that the Austrians, who were already occupying Tuscany and the northern part of the Papal States, would soon be threatening Rome itself. There was no time to lose: he could benefit from the situation by restoring the Pope and winning the approval of the Church which would follow from this.

The French Assembly agreed to Napoleon's plan of providing an **expeditionary force** to be sent to Rome, and 10,000 troops set sail in April 1849. Their commander was well received when they landed in the Papal States near Rome and confidently expected a similar welcome from the citizens of Rome itself. He was not prepared for the strong resistance organised by Mazzini and Garibaldi. Louis Napoleon then agreed to an armistice, but only to buy time. A Bonaparte could not begin his presidency of France with a military defeat or a meek compromise. Hence, he reinforced his army, and soon over 20,000 French soldiers attacked. Rome fell in July.

The consequences

In a sense, Napoleon had succeeded. Papal rule had been restored, as he intended, the Austrians had been kept at bay, and at home he received support from **clericalist** forces. Yet the heir of the revolutionary Napoleon Bonaparte had made himself the champion of the most illiberal regime in Europe, that of Pope Pius IX, and Rome was quickly restored to the reactionary government of the papal governing body, the Curia.

The government of Rome was again as it had been: backward and oppressive. There were loud complaints in the French assembly at this betrayal of republican principles. What is more, Napoleon himself realised that he had made a grave error. His first action in foreign policy had been to restore the temporal power of the papacy, which he himself, in 1830, had tried to remove. Such an action was unworthy of a Bonaparte. He would have to achieve more worthy successes in the future.

'Doing something for Italy'

In December 1852 Napoleon assumed the title of Emperor Napoleon III. He declared that France wanted peace, but quickly found himself fighting against

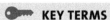

Russia in defence of Turkey in the Crimean War, which broke out in 1854. Among France's allies was Piedmont, and when the war ended, in 1856, Cavour too had a seat at the peace conference in Paris. This brought the two men into close contact, with important long-term consequences for them both. After the conference ended, they kept in touch through mutual friends and through Napoleon's nephew, a doctor who treated them both, Cavour's private secretary, and the young and beautiful **Countess Castiglione**.

On a number of occasions in the 1850s Napoleon spoke to Cavour about 'doing something for Italy' but did not explain what that something might be. It is difficult to know what, if anything, he had in mind. Certainly, if he had any plans, they were at this stage vague and capable of being changed at any moment. And, of course, they were secret, making it doubly difficult to unravel them.

Napoleon III's motives

It may be that, as a romantic but sincere supporter of Italian independence, Napoleon wished to be helpful to the cause. Although he had none of the qualities, the determination and the gifts of leadership that Napoleon I had possessed, he saw himself as a leader of 'the peoples of Europe' in their search for freedom and national identity. As for the episode of the Roman Republic in 1849, that was best forgotten.

Yet it is very easy to see an element of self-interest in Napoleon's views. After all, a pro-Italian policy was by its very nature anti-Austrian, and Austria, as the leading conservative power in Europe, was the natural enemy of France. Furthermore, although Napoleon wished to drive the Austrians out of northern Italy and thereby strengthen Piedmont, he wished to keep the growth of Piedmont within bounds. The new Piedmont, although large enough to be a useful ally for France, should not become so large as to act independently of France, to oppose French wishes or to be a threat to France itself. It must certainly not be allowed to become strong enough to interfere with French ambitions to acquire Nice and Savoy. The return of these areas, once part of Napoleon I's territory, would be a tangible sign of his success. According to his critics, Napoleon III simply wished to replace Austrian influence in Italy with French, and thus he was more a French imperialist than a true supporter of Italian nationalism – a criticism that had also been levelled against his uncle.

We also have to ask what Napoleon III meant when he talked about 'Italy'. Some historians believe that, before 1861, 'Italy' to him meant northern Italy, the old Napoleonic Kingdom of Italy, made up of states such as Piedmont, already substantially French in character as a consequence of the occupying forces at the beginning of the century, and where French was still the language of the educated minority. At this stage it is doubtful whether Napoleon would have wanted the whole Italian peninsula united into a single kingdom. After all, such a united country might become a threat to France itself.

 **KEY FIGURE**

Virginia di Castiglione (1837–99)

A 19-year-old whom Cavour sent to Paris to seduce the emperor. Napoleon slept with her, considering her 'very pretty but with no charm'.

SOURCE F

What propaganda message of Napoleon III was Source F intended to convey?

An 1852 painting of Napoleon III on horseback.

What of central Italy? This could become part of the new Piedmont or a separate French-controlled state, perhaps governed by one of Napoleon's many cousins. Other cousins could rule Naples and Sicily. The Pope would be persuaded to agree to all these arrangements by being made president of an Italian Federation of States (see page 61).

This scenario seemed to Napoleon a splendid idea which would appeal to almost everyone. It might well have been Napoleon's ideal solution to the Italian question. But would the French emperor be motivated enough to attempt to make it a reality?

The Orsini affair

Napoleon moved into action in January 1858, after an attempt was made on his life. A group of four Italians, led by Count **Felice Orsini**, was responsible. Orsini had been a refugee in London, where he had had three large bombs specially made for him. The men took the bombs from London to Paris via Brussels, by train, completely outwitting the French police who had been tipped off that they would be arriving by road. The bombs were thrown at Napoleon and the Empress Eugénie as their coach arrived at the opera. Eight people died and about 150 were injured, but the emperor and his wife were unharmed.

Orsini seems to have believed that, if he killed Napoleon, a new republican government in France would come to the assistance of Italy. At his trial, a letter, said to have been written by Orsini in his prison cell, was read out. In the letter, Orsini appealed to Napoleon to help Italy to achieve independence and by doing so to receive the blessing of 25 million Italian citizens. There is some evidence that Napoleon himself encouraged Orsini to write this letter and may even have dictated its contents. He certainly arranged for it to be published. Perhaps he was genuinely impressed by Orsini's letter. Perhaps he feared that, unless he took action, further assassination attempts might be made. Perhaps he just saw the opportunity to gain prestige. What is certain, however, is that Napoleon now decided to do something for Italy, and for France.

Napoleon met Cavour at Plombières on 21 July 1858 (see pages 60–2). All that was needed was a suitable pretext for war.

KEY FIGURE

Felice Orsini (1819–58)
An Italian patriot and follower of Mazzini. He had been elected a member of the Roman assembly in 1848 and, under Garibaldi, had taken part in the defence of the city against the French. He was executed after the assassination attempt.

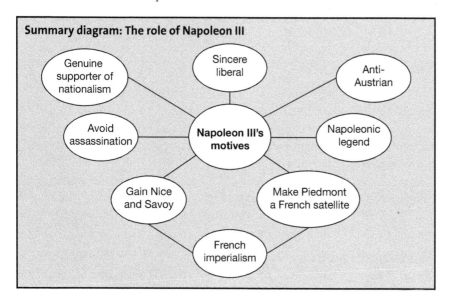

Summary diagram: The role of Napoleon III

- Genuine supporter of nationalism
- Sincere liberal
- Anti-Austrian
- Avoid assassination
- **Napoleon III's motives**
- Napoleonic legend
- Gain Nice and Savoy
- Make Piedmont a French satellite
- French imperialism

The war of 1859

> ▶ *In what ways, and to what extent, did the war of 1859 further the cause of Italian unification?*
>
> ▶ *How favourable to Piedmont were developments in 1859–60?*

Preparations for war

After Plombières and the secret treaty, Cavour began to prepare Italians psychologically for war by writing an emotional anti-Austrian speech for Victor Emmanuel to give at the opening of parliament in January 1859. This included the words, 'We cannot be insensitive to the cry of anguish [*grido di dolore*] that comes to us from many parts of Italy'. '*Grido di dolore*' quickly became a catchphrase throughout Italy to express popular anti-Austrian feelings. Nationalistic emotion was heightened.

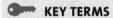 **KEY TERMS**

Mobilised Organised for a possible war.

Congress A meeting of several countries to settle key issues.

Cavour also **mobilised** the Piedmontese army in March 1859. But without Louis Napoleon's support, he could not risk fighting alone against Austria. There must be no repetition of Piedmont's defeat by Austria at the battles of Custoza and Novara, just over a decade earlier.

Yet still war did not begin, and there were signs that Napoleon was beginning to get cold feet. Unless Austria could be made to appear the aggressor, he reasoned, it might be better to abandon the idea of war and turn instead to a **congress** of the Great Powers to settle the Italian question, an idea which displeased Cavour. He feared that Piedmont would not find a place at such a conference and would be considered 'feeble and powerless' by the rest of Italy. But all he could do was express his hope to the French emperor that Austria 'will before long commit one of those aggressive acts which will justify your armed intervention. I hope so with all my heart.' In other words, he was hoping that something would turn up.

Declarations of war

In April 1859 something did turn up. Austria issued a demand that Piedmont should demobilise its army. The Austrians themselves had mobilised a large army in northern Italy the previous month, fearing a possible attack, and they could not afford the expense of keeping it at the ready for very long. They dared not disband while Piedmont still had an army ready for war, and so took the dangerous step of sending the ultimatum. Cavour refused to comply and Victor Emmanuel issued a proclamation: 'People of Italy! Austria provokes Piedmont … I fight for the right of the whole nation … I have no other ambition than to be the first soldier of Italian independence.'

Austria replied by declaring war on 29 April 1859. A few days later Napoleon declared support for his ally. The war known to the Italians as 'the Second War of Independence' – the first being that fought against the Austrians in 1849 – had begun. It was a short, violent and terrible conflict.

The battles

The war started slowly, marked by chaos, confusion and unpreparedness on both sides. Napoleon's troops travelled to Italy by train, as befitted a modern army; but, owing to bad organisation, they arrived in Lombardy before their equipment and provisions. 'We have sent an army of 120,000 men into Italy before we have stocked up supplies', Napoleon complained to Paris. There were not enough tents for the men and, even worse, there was not enough ammunition. The only consolation was that the Austrian and Piedmontese generals were even more incompetent, so that it was some time before fighting could actually begin.

Lombardy was quickly overrun by French and Piedmontese forces. The Austrians were defeated at Magenta on 4 June, by the French army, and at Solferino on 24 June, by a combined French–Piedmontese force. (See the map on page 71.) The carnage at both battles and on both sides was horrific.

The Austrian emperor, Victor Emmanuel and Napoleon, all present as spectators, were deeply shocked. 'Better to lose a province than undergo such a horrible experience again', mused the young Austrian emperor, Franz Joseph. Napoleon offered his personal linen to be torn up as bandages for his men, but this gesture hardly compensated the wounded for the fact that the official bandages, along with the medical and other supplies, did not arrive until after the war was over. Hence, many who were terribly maimed often lay for hours on the battlefield without any help, until death ended their suffering. The local peasantry stripped the boots from the bodies of dead and dying alike. At Solferino, the French lost almost 12,000 men, the Austrians even more.

The only good thing to come out of this useless slaughter was the arrival on the battlefield of the Swiss journalist Henry Dunant, whose reports of the horrors led eventually to the formation of the **Red Cross** organisation.

The settlement

The war was mercifully short – only seven weeks – because Napoleon suddenly made a truce with Austria. In August he met Franz Joseph at Villafranca and agreed an armistice. He did not consult his Piedmontese allies over the terms. He simply informed King Victor Emmanuel what they were, and the king accepted them without consulting Cavour.

According to the terms of this agreement:

- Piedmont would receive Lombardy, although, to allow Austria to save face, it would first be **ceded** to France and then passed by Napoleon to Victor Emmanuel.

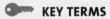 **KEY TERMS**

Red Cross An international agency founded in 1864 to assist those who were wounded or captured in wars.

Ceded Officially handed over.

- The previous rulers of Tuscany, Modena and Parma, who had fled when revolts had broken out in their lands, were to be restored to their Duchies. (This was the theory, although it was not clear how it was to be achieved, and it soon became apparent that they would never return.)
- Austria still kept Venetia and therefore remained a powerful influence in Italy.

SOURCE G

In what ways does Source G show that the British cartoonist is biased against France?

THE GIANT AND THE DWARF.

"BRAVO, MY LITTLE FELLOW! YOU SHALL DO ALL THE FIGHTING, AND WE'LL DIVIDE THE GLORY!"

'The Giant and the Dwarf.' A cartoon from *Punch*, a British satirical magazine, 11 June 1859, representing Napoleon III (on the left) and a diminutive Victor Emmanuel II.

Napoleon's motives

Why did Napoleon make his sudden and unexpected truce with Austria in July and then, without consulting Cavour, agree to the armistice of Villafranca? There are many possibilities, and the answer probably lies in a combination of them:

- As a military leader, Napoleon had not the stomach for war. The battles of Magenta and Solferino, with their great loss of life, affected him severely. He may well have felt that by bringing the war to an early end he could at least prevent another such bloodbath.
- The Austrians had been defeated but not routed. Their forces had withdrawn into the stronghold of the **'quadrilateral'**. There was thus little hope that what was left of the French and Piedmontese armies could breach the Austrian defences. Reinforcements would be needed, and obtaining these would take time, and casualties in a further round of fighting would be high.
- There was danger too that Prussia, already mobilising along the Rhine frontier, might take advantage of Napoleon's absence to attack France. Alternatively, Prussia might decide to come to the aid of Austria if the war were allowed to continue, and a combined Prusso-Austrian army might prove invincible.
- In France itself, there was growing criticism of the whole Italian adventure and Napoleon was becoming increasingly suspicious of Cavour's activities. In Tuscany the Grand Duke had left his Duchy and gone to Vienna, and

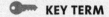
KEY TERM

Quadrilateral A group of four heavily defended fortresses near the Austrian border (in Mantua, Peschiera, Verona and Legnago).

In what ways would the map soon be altered, as a result of the war in 1859?

Figure 3.1 Northern and central Italy 1848–59.

a provisional government had announced that it wished Tuscany to be united with Piedmont. Revolution had spread to Modena and Parma, where Piedmontese armies moved in and took over, setting up provisional governments, while Cavour's agents were known to be encouraging revolution in the Papal States. It seemed to Napoleon that Piedmont was trying to gain more territory and more power than had been agreed at Plombières.

The resignation of Cavour

Napoleon III considered that Piedmont was doing well – indeed too well – out of the war. On the other hand, the French emperor himself, aware that he had not, as promised at Plombières, driven Austria out of Italy, could not yet demand Nice and Savoy as his share of the spoils.

Nevertheless, Cavour felt that he had been badly led down. He disliked the fact that Austria still controlled Venetia, and was appalled with the supposed arrangement in Tuscany, Modena and Parma. He was also furious that he had not been consulted over the ending of the war. Generally a calm, reasonable man who knew the importance of compromise, Cavour also had a furious temper. In a hysterical interview with Victor Emmanuel, in which he appeared to lose control of himself, he insisted that Piedmont should continue the war against Austria without French aid. When the king, very sensibly, refused, he resigned as prime minister.

An expanded Piedmont

Cavour was out of office for the next nine months. Yet the situation turned out to be far better for Piedmont than he had imagined. His work as prime minister had borne fruit. Piedmont may not have extended its influence quite as quickly as he had hoped, but the growth in its power was unmistakable:

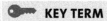

KEY TERM

Annexation The act of taking possession of land and adding it to one's own territory.

- In Tuscany, a carefully rigged assembly voted unanimously in August for **annexation** by Piedmont.
- So too did Modena, Parma and the Romagna in the Papal States. Because of the expected opposition of Napoleon, however, these unions were not immediately put into effect. Instead, provisional, pro-Piedmontese governments were left in control in each of them.
- The Armistice of Villafranca developed into a peace conference held in Zurich in November, and this time Piedmont was invited to send representatives. The Peace of Zurich arranged that Lombardy was to be handed over, first by Austria to France and then by Napoleon to Piedmont. The problems of central Italy were shelved, to be dealt with by one of Napoleon III's favourite methods, a Congress, although objections from the Pope – who feared that he would lose territory in the Papal States – meant that it never took place.

Hence, when Cavour returned as prime minister, he was able to put the final touches to Piedmont's expansion or, from another perspective, to the unification of northern Italy.

Annexation of Tuscany and Emilia

In mid-March 1860 in Tuscany the population voted for union with Piedmont. Despite Villafranca, the new state of Emilia (made up of the Duchies of Modena and Parma, together with the Romagna) (see the map on page 110) did the same. This was in fact a foregone conclusion: the war against Austria had whipped up nationalist feelings and the provisional governments had carried out extensive propaganda campaigns:

- In Tuscany, 386,445 voted for annexation, and 14,925 against.
- In Emilia, 427,512 voted for annexation, and 756 voted against.

In Turin decrees were published declaring Tuscany and Emilia part of the Kingdom of Piedmont.

Nice and Savoy

By this time Cavour realised that one way to restore good relations with Napoleon was to arrange for Nice and Savoy to be handed over to him without further delay. A secret treaty between Victor Emmanuel and Napoleon in March transferred Savoy and Nice to France, subject to the results of a popular vote in both places. These votes were taken in April and again huge majorities voted in favour of union:

- In Savoy, 130,583 were for, with 235 against.
- In Nice, 24,448 were for, with 160 against.

The result in French-speaking Savoy was not unexpected, but in Nice, which was Italian speaking, the vote were suspicious. The presence of a French army in Nice on its way home from Lombardy may have had something to do with it.

Among those who questioned the accuracy of the results was Garibaldi, who had been born in Nice and was one of its elected representatives in the Piedmontese parliament. The transfer of Nice to the French, he later recalled, made him feel 'a foreigner in the land of my birth'. He was preparing a military expedition to prevent Nice being taken over by France when he was diverted by an outbreak of revolution in southern Italy on the island of Sicily.

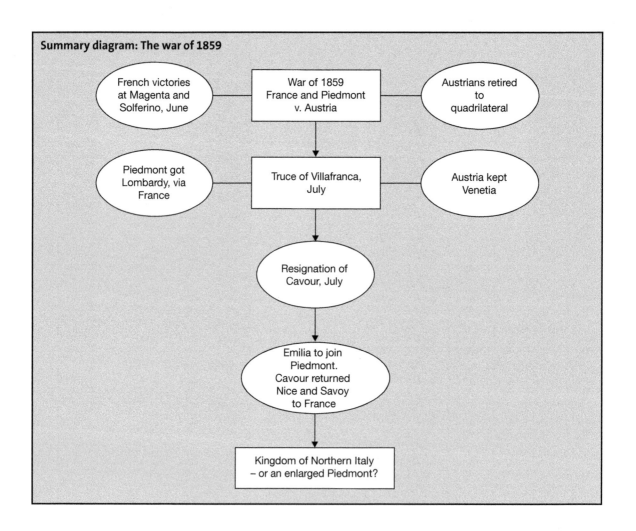

Summary diagram: The war of 1859

- French victories at Magenta and Solferino, June
- War of 1859 France and Piedmont v. Austria
- Austrians retired to quadrilateral
- Piedmont got Lombardy, via France
- Truce of Villafranca, July
- Austria kept Venetia
- Resignation of Cavour, July
- Emilia to join Piedmont. Cavour returned Nice and Savoy to France
- Kingdom of Northern Italy – or an enlarged Piedmont?

5 Cavour and Garibaldi

▶ *Why did disagreements between Cavour and Garibaldi affect the political/military situation in 1859–60?*

▶ *How did Cavour and Garibaldi differ in their personalities, aims and tactics?*

Historians have argued for a long time about the motives of Cavour and Garibaldi and about the relations between the two men. Their own writings are not much help. Cavour died without writing an autobiography. He did send a large number of letters, but these were 'edited' after his death – with some items being suppressed and others simply invented – to show him in an unrealistically good light. Garibaldi did write memoirs but only covering the period up to 1850, and they are generally unreliable.

Both Cavour and Garibaldi were born in Piedmont, and both played leading roles in the unification of Italy. But there the similarity ends. The two men were highly contrasting figures. Cavour was a nobleman – well educated, intelligent, outwardly cool, calm and collected – as well as the fat little politician and diplomat. Garibaldi was a rough, ill-educated soldier and leader of men.

Ready to take chances at any time, passionate and charismatic, Garibaldi had ideas that were simple and straightforward, and he did not allow them to get in the way of action. He had come under the influence of Mazzini in 1831 and, although he afterwards abandoned republican ideals, becoming instead a monarchist and following Piedmont's king, Victor Emmanuel II, he always retained his nationalist beliefs and continued to fight for an independent and united Italy. All his actions were aimed at driving out Austria, the foreigner, from Italian soil and establishing an Italian kingdom under the rule of Piedmont. These aims became an obsession which dominated his life and dictated almost his every action.

Cavour was altogether more cautious. He had written in the 1830s about the *possibility* of a united Italy, but even at the time of the Plombières meeting with Napoleon in 1858 he was not fully committed to the idea of a united Italy.

Cavour's tactics

Cavour was realistic enough to know that '*Italia farà da sè*' ('Italy will make herself by herself'), as Charles Albert had hoped (see page 52), was an impossible aim. There was no hope of Piedmont being able to expel Austria from northern Italy without outside help, and the only available source of help was Napoleon and the French army. Cavour had reasoned that France would be prepared to help, at least up to a point, in return for Nice and Savoy, but he also realised that Napoleon would not agree to unlimited expansion for Piedmont and would not wish Piedmont to become the leader of a united Italy. After all, an Italy of separate states could be useful to France in any conflict with Austria, while a truly united Italy might become a possible threat to France herself. It was probably not until Napoleon accepted Piedmont's acquisition of Tuscany and Emilia in early 1860 that Cavour saw greater possibilities.

Even then, he does not seem to have been convinced that a totally united Italy was either possible or desirable. Piedmont had gained control over northern Italy by diplomacy and limited war; anything more in the way of territorial gains might involve a disastrous civil war. For him it was time to stop. Not so for Garibaldi.

Garibaldi's boldness

Garibaldi wanted Rome, Venetia, Naples and Sicily, as part of a united Italy, and he wanted them at once. In 1860 he undertook a military expedition to Sicily to unite southern Italy with Piedmont by revolution. His expedition and its results are dealt with in Chapter 4 (see pages 91–6).

Cavour's motives

It is difficult to know what Cavour thought of Garibaldi's plan. Some historians – especially those who tend to stress the glorious nature of the *Risorgimento* and to see the leading figures as working together to produce unification – believe that Cavour pretended to stop Garibaldi while secretly supporting him. This may have been because he thought of Garibaldi as an ally or because he intended from the start to use Garibaldi for his own purposes.

Other historians – stressing the unpredictable nature of events and seeing the leading figures as fundamentally opposed – see Cavour as Garibaldi's enemy, opposed to his plans for unification. He pretended to support the expedition to Sicily, partly because he feared that open opposition might lead to a loss of popular support for the government in Piedmont's elections; but secretly he worked to make it fail. These historians believe that he disliked the whole idea of Garibaldi's expedition to attack Sicily and Naples.

'I omitted nothing to persuade Garibaldi to drop his mad scheme', wrote Cavour just before Garibaldi set out for Sicily in April 1860. There is little doubt that Cavour disliked the man, thinking him stupid and probably untrustworthy. Garibaldi had been a republican and had only lately become a royalist. Cavour was not entirely sure whether this change of heart was genuine. If he were successful in the south, might he possibly demand a republican Italy? If so, this would, he thought, at best lead to a divided country, with a republic in the south and a monarchy in the north.

On 12 July 1860 Cavour complained privately that Garibaldi was 'planning the wildest, not to say absurdest, schemes'. But when it became clear, in early August, that the expedition to Sicily had been successful, he changed his tune completely. Now he insisted that Garibaldi 'has done the greatest service that a man can do; he has given the Italians self-confidence; he has proved to Europe that Italians can fight and die in battle to reconquer a fatherland.'

At this stage Cavour probably believed that unification was inevitable. He added that 'If, in spite of all our efforts, he should liberate southern Italy as he liberated Sicily, we would have no choice but to go along with him.'

Most historians now favour the interpretation that Italy was unified as a result of the clash of Garibaldi and Cavour, rather than by their working in harmony. Yet the attempt to pluck out the secret motives of historical characters is always hazardous. We are on safer ground in reconstructing what they actually did and in assessing the results of their actions.

Success in southern Italy

When, against all expectations, Garibaldi's expedition to Sicily had proved successful by the end of July 1860, Cavour had to decide how to react. He called for the annexation of Sicily by Piedmont. There were difficulties, however, for while the Sicilians wanted independence from Naples they certainly did not want to replace Naples with Piedmont. Then came news that Garibaldi and his men had crossed to the mainland on 19 August and were marching north towards Naples.

Cavour may have thought that France and perhaps also Austria – both Catholic powers – would intervene if Garibaldi's army proceeded from Naples into the Papal States. France had kept a garrison in Rome since the days of the Roman Republic (see page 40). Any attack on the city therefore would certainly lead to conflict. Cavour was also worried about the growing popularity of Garibaldi, not only in Sicily but also in Piedmont and throughout Italy. Might he even lead a revolution and take control in Piedmont, or indeed in the whole of Italy?

Cavour decided that he must act:

- First, he tried to stir up pro-Piedmontese risings in Naples, before Garibaldi entered the city. But these failed, and Garibaldi's army continued its northward progress.
- Cavour then became bolder. He decided to organise an invasion of the Papal States from the north to block Garibaldi's army, which was invading from the south, before it could reach Rome and the Pope.

The invading Piedmontese troops were not well received in the Papal States and met considerable opposition from the civilian population on their way south to stop Garibaldi's army. But, in a secret agreement, Napoleon III agreed, though breaking off diplomatic relations with Piedmont, that he would in effect turn a blind eye to the invasion, so long as Rome itself was untouched. Hence, Cavour was free to defeat the opposition. As for Garibaldi's forces, they were successful against the Neapolitan forces, winning a victory on 18 September; but their progress further north was barred by a Piedmontese army led by Victor Emmanuel II.

On 26 October Garibaldi and Victor Emmanuel, at the head of their two armies, met at Teano. But there was no showdown. Garibaldi simply agreed to hand over the territories he controlled to the king (see page 95). Almost all of southern and central Italy came under the effective control of the Kingdom of Piedmont. Cavour's gamble on invading the Papal States had paid off, and made the unification of Italy under the leadership of Piedmont and the government of Victor Emmanuel a reality.

The Kingdom of Italy

Cavour had arranged for the people of Naples and afterwards of Sicily to vote whether or not there should be a united Italy under Victor Emmanuel. Organising the voting was particularly difficult in Sicily, where most of population was illiterate and did not understand the Italian of the north. Difficulties were allegedly overcome by providing each voter with two voting slips, one saying 'yes' and the other 'no', and by having two ballot boxes similarly marked. Unfortunately, even those who could read had no idea who or what Victor Emmanuel was. Even the word 'Italia', which had been Garibaldi's slogan during the fighting, merely confused Sicilians further. Union with Piedmont was not mentioned. In fact, most people probably assumed, quite simply, that they were voting for the end of the feudal monarchy of the Bourbons. Nevertheless, their overwhelming vote in favour of change – with 99.2 per cent in Naples and 99.8 per cent in Sicily voting yes – meant that they had opted for union under Piedmont's Victor Emmanuel II.

Voting also took place in November 1860 in the eastern and central parts of the Papal States occupied by Piedmont, and again enormous numbers voted for union with Piedmont. This time 99.3 per cent were reported to be in favour.

In March 1861 the Kingdom of Italy was proclaimed, with Victor Emmanuel II as King of Italy. Not quite all of the peninsula was now part of the new kingdom: the 'Patrimony of St Peter', the area around Rome, remained under the control of the Pope and in French occupation, and Venetia remained in Austrian hands. Everywhere else unification was complete and under the control of Piedmont.

Cavour did not live to see a fully united and independent Italy. He died in March 1861 from 'a fever'.

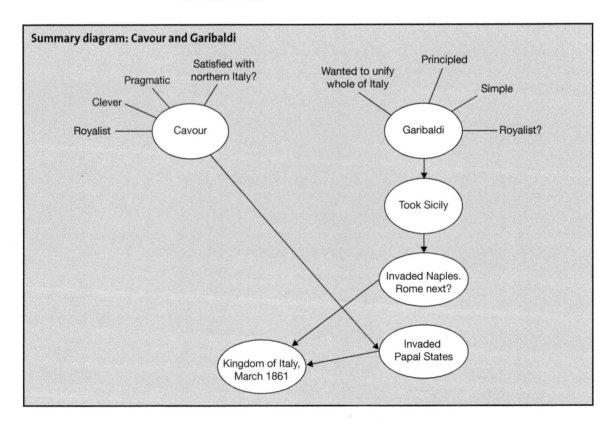

Summary diagram: Cavour and Garibaldi

Chapter summary

In 1815, when Victor Emmanuel I returned as an absolute monarch to Piedmont after the Napoleonic upheavals, there seemed little likelihood that his state would spearhead Italian unification. Yet in 1848 widespread unrest convinced King Charles Albert to introduce a new constitution (the *Statuto*) that helped to create greater political freedom than elsewhere in Italy, and at the same time he attempted to defeat the Austrians in northern Italy and expand Piedmont's control. He was badly defeated at Custoza and then Novara; but in the following decade Piedmont became much stronger economically and in Cavour, premier from 1852, it found a supremely able figure who was determined to destroy Austrian influence in Italy.

First by joining the Crimean War and then by doing a deal with the French Emperor at Plombières in 1858, Cavour prepared the ground for a war by Piedmont and its French ally against Austria. The result was victory in 1859. This did not give Cavour all he wanted, but he was able to utilise nationalistic feeling to create a new kingdom in northern Italy. Unification of the whole peninsula followed, though due more to the exploits of Garibaldi in Sicily and Naples than to Cavour's plans.

Refresher questions

Use these questions to remind yourself of the key material covered in this chapter.

1 Why did Victor Emmanuel I abdicate in 1821?

2 In what ways was Charles Albert an illiberal ruler of Piedmont?

3 In what ways was Charles Albert progressive?

4 What were the main provisions of the *Statuto*?

5 How far did the *Statuto* fall below the demands of the reformers, and how far did it advance politics in Piedmont?

6 Why was Piedmont, in the 1850s, the state most likely to spearhead Italian unification?

7 Why did Charles Albert fail in his attempts to defeat Austrian forces in 1848–9?

8 How successful in domestic affairs was Cavour as prime minister?

9 What was the significance of Piedmont's participation in the Crimean War?

10 What was decided at Plombières?

11 What were Napoleon III's motives in fighting against Austria in 1859 and then in ending the war?

12 Who was the more realistic: Cavour, in wanting to carry on the war against Austria after the withdrawal of French support, or Victor Emmanuel II, in refusing to do so?

13 By what process did the victory against Austria lead to the creation of the Kingdom of Northern Italy?

14 Why was Cavour so hostile to Garibaldi?

15 How important a role did Cavour play in the unification of Italy?

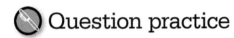
Question practice

ESSAY QUESTIONS

1 How successful a prime minister of Piedmont was Cavour from 1852 to 1861?

2 Which of the following was the more important factor in the unification of Italy? i) The diplomacy of Cavour. ii) The military exploits of Garibaldi. Explain your answer with reference to both i) and ii).

3 How far did Cavour's actions contribute to the unification of Italy in the period 1852–9?

4 How far do you agree that Cavour's primary aim in 1852–61 was the unification of northern Italy?

INTERPRETATION QUESTION

1 Read the interpretation and then answer the question that follows. 'More convincing is the view he [Cavour] united Italy not so much as the result of intention or conviction but more through force of circumstances.' (From *The Unification of Italy*, A. Stiles, 2006.) Evaluate the strengths and limitations of this interpretation, making reference to other interpretations you have studied.

SOURCE ANALYSIS QUESTIONS

1 How much weight do you give the evidence of Source 1 for an enquiry into Victor Emmanuel's aims and achievements as king of Piedmont? Explain your answer using the source, the information given about it and your own knowledge of the historical context.

2 How far could the historian make use of Sources 2 and 3 together (page 81) to investigate the roles of Napoleon III and Cavour in fostering the unification of northern Italy? Explain your answer using both sources, the information you have about them and your own knowledge of the historical context.

SOURCE I

From the French ambassador in Piedmont to the French foreign minister, 16 October 1852, quoted in Denis Mack Smith, *The Making of Italy, 1796–1866*, Palgrave Macmillan, 1988, pp. 170–1.

Victor Emmanuel is in no sense a liberal: his tastes, his education, and his whole habit of behaviour all go the other way. He tells everyone that 'my father bestowed institutions on the country which are quite unfitted to its needs and the temper of its inhabitants'. To some people he will add, 'but my father and myself have both given our word, and I will not break it'. To others, however, he will say confidentially, 'I am only waiting for the right moment to change everything. The moment will be the outbreak of war. Whenever it comes, I shall be ready.' Any French official who finds himself alone with the King will be asked if the time has yet arrived …

King Victor Emmanuel, I repeat, does not like the existing constitution, nor does he like parliamentary liberties, nor a free press.

SOURCE 2

From Cavour's speech to parliament in 1855, quoted in Edward Henry Nolan, *The Liberators of Italy: Or, the Lives of Garibaldi; Victor Emmanuel, King of Italy; Count Cavour; and Napoleon III, Emperor of the French*, James S. Virtue, 1864, p. 274.

The sons of Italy can fight with true valour on the field of glory … I am sure that the laurels our soldiers will win on the battlefields of the east will do more for the future of Italy than all those who have thought to revive her with the voice and with the pen … so that she can take her rightful place among the Great Powers.

SOURCE 3

From a letter written to Victor Emmanuel in July 1858, quoted in Denis Mack Smith, *The Making of Italy*, Palgrave Macmillan, 1988, pp. 238–47.

As soon as I entered the Emperor's study, he raised the question which was the purpose of my journey. He began by saying that he had decided to support Piedmont with all his power in a war against Austria, provided that the war was undertaken for a non-revolutionary end which could be justified in the eyes of diplomatic circles, and still more in the eyes of French and European public opinion.

CHAPTER 4

Garibaldi and Italy

This chapter focuses on the life and achievements of just one man, the controversial Giuseppe Garibaldi. The material is divided into the following sections:

★ Garibaldi's early career 1807–49

★ Garibaldi and 'The Thousand'

★ Garibaldi and Rome

★ Garibaldi: an assessment

Was Garibaldi a brave adventurer and a natural leader of men who led a remarkably colourful life, or was he more: the only true patriot of the *Risorgimento* who devoted his life to the cause of Italian nationhood? The balanced conclusion reached by most historians was that he was a mixture of both. Do you agree? Do not give undue attention to his eccentricities and fitful lifestyle; instead, concentrate on his successes and failures, and estimate his importance to the unification of Italy.

Key dates

1807		Garibaldi was born in Nice	1859		Garibaldi returned to Piedmont and became a wholehearted supporter of Victor Emmanuel II
1815		Nice became part of Piedmont			
1831		Garibaldi met Mazzini and became a nationalist	1860	May 11	Garibaldi landed in Sicily
1833		Garibaldi was sentenced to death in his absence for his part in an unsuccessful revolutionary plot in Piedmont		May	Garibaldi took control of Sicily
				Oct. 26	Garibaldi agreed that Victor Emmanuel should control Naples and Sicily
1848		Garibaldi returned to Italy from South America and became a royalist	1862	Aug.	Garibaldi was defeated at Aspromonte
			1867	Nov. 3	Garibaldi was defeated at Mentana
1849	July 3	The Roman Republic fell	1882		Death of Garibaldi, aged 75

1 Garibaldi's early career 1807–49

▶ *Why did Garibaldi switch from being a republican to a royalist?*
▶ *How did Garibaldi achieve great popularity in Italy?*

Today, in Britain, the name Garibaldi is hardly remembered at all, except perhaps as the name of a currant biscuit; but in Victorian England it was a name to conjure with. Garibaldi was the swashbuckling adventurer, the national patriot, the leader of men, who had struck a blow for freedom in Italy.

On a state visit to Britain in 1864 he was greeted with enormous enthusiasm by the largest crowds seen in London for many years, all of whom wanted to touch his hand as he rode in a state procession. During the drive he was greeted with a great deal more applause and excitement than Queen Victoria, who accompanied him, very much to Her Majesty's annoyance. Soon afterwards his visit was cut short, almost certainly on royal orders. 'Garibaldi – thank God – has gone!' noted Victoria in her journal. Others, however, were not so happy. The servants at Stafford House, where he had stayed, are alleged to have made a small fortune by selling bottles of soapsuds said to have come from his washbasin. He was without doubt one of the most famous people in the world at this time, a veritable media superstar. His image, in portraits and photographs reproduced as cheap prints and in magazines, seemed to be everywhere. A popular cult of personality had grown up around him, celebrating, retelling and sometimes distorting his achievements.

Giuseppe Garibaldi's life was, by any standards, colourful and dramatic. He himself described it as having been tempestuous, made up of unusual amounts of good and evil.

Early life

Giuseppe Garibaldi was born a French citizen in Nice in 1807, but he was only eight years old when Nice became part of Piedmont after the Congress of Vienna in 1815. In any case, both his parents were Italian and he always thought of himself as Italian. His father was a sailor and, despite his family's wishes that he should enter the Church, Garibaldi followed his father and at the age of fifteen joined the **merchant navy**. It was as a result of this that a chance encounter in Marseilles in 1831 brought him into contact with Mazzini and altered his life forever.

Disciple of Mazzini

Mazzini, the founder of 'Young Italy' (see page 29), believed that Italy should be free, independent and united, with the people having a say in government, and

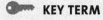

KEY TERM

Merchant navy A country's commercial shipping fleet.

that a republic was more likely than a monarchy to bring this about. Mazzini's greatest gift was probably to inspire revolutionary leaders with nationalist fervour and patriotic enthusiasm, and the greatest of his disciples was Garibaldi.

Garibaldi was quickly converted to the dream of a united Italy, joined the 'Young Italy' movement, and in 1833 became involved in Mazzini's revolutionary plans in Piedmont. The plot, intended to start a mutiny in the army and navy, went wrong, and Garibaldi was among those sentenced to death for their part in the scheme.

South American interlude

Fortunately for Garibaldi, he had already left the country before the trial began and so the sentence could not be carried out. Signing on as second mate, he sailed for South America, where he stayed for a dozen years, settling first in Rio de Janeiro. There he found that a branch of 'Young Italy' was already established. He joined and quickly became involved in revolutionary plans. Planning, though, was not enough for him. He wanted action and for a while he became a pirate preying on the shipping of the New World, and then he joined a rebel army in Brazil. In between campaigns he found time to fall in love and run away with a fisherman's wife who became his devoted, insanely jealous companion for the next ten years.

After six years of fighting, Garibaldi moved to Montevideo in Uruguay and adopted the humdrum life of a commercial traveller selling spaghetti. He quickly became bored by this, however, and joined the army defending Uruguay against an Argentinean takeover. He raised an Italian legion of **guerrilla fighters** which fought with much bravery if little skill, and was largely responsible for the final Uruguayan victory.

It was during this time that Garibaldi's **Legion** wore the famous red shirt for the first time. This was originally modelled on the South American **poncho**, and Garibaldi had seen it being worn by local slaughtermen. It was cheap and easy to make and, being red in colour, did not show the blood – of either cattle or men. Later, inspired by the uniform of the New York Fire Brigade, Garibaldi introduced sleeves, and then brass buttons, making the whole design much more like that of a shirt. After his return with his legionaries to Italy, the manufacture of these shirts was willingly undertaken by young seamstresses sympathetic to his cause (as shown in Source A below).

Instead of the red shirt, Garibaldi himself sometimes wore a white poncho, a relic of his South American days, and his portraits – including that by Saverio Altamura (see Source B below) – show him with a circle-brimmed hat tipped over one eye. His shapeless trousers were homemade by himself, but as he never mastered buttonholes they had to be tied up with laces. He preferred a simple life and ate little. Rather rough in manner, he was generally good humoured, but could be ruthless and determined. His main interests were fighting and women.

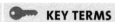

KEY TERMS

Guerrilla fighters Small independent groups, using unorthodox tactics, fighting against regular troops.

Legion The name taken by Garibaldi's irregular troops. Originally it was a division of 3000–6000 men in the army of Ancient Rome. Individual members were called legionaries.

Poncho A circular cape-like garment with no sleeves or fastenings, and merely a hole for the head.

SOURCE A

'The Seamstresses of the Red Shirts' (1863) by Odoardo Borrani. Note the portrait of Garibaldi on the wall (lower right).

What may have motivated the seamstresses who made the famous Red Shirts, as depicted in Source A?

He 'collected' a large number of women over the years in addition to the three he married.

Scandal and gossip followed him, but could not hide his success as a leader of soldiers or his devotion to the cause of Italian unity.

On his return to Italy in 1848 he was to inspire great devotion from his men, and, after his heroic defence of the Roman Republic, a near-religious adoration from ordinary people. Street songs, ballads and popular prints of the time show him as semi-divine. In effect a local patron saint, his portrait was displayed in a place of honour next to that of the Madonna in Italian homes. Many found his charisma quite overwhelming.

SOURCE B

What is there about the image in Source B that Italians found appealing?

A contemporary portrait of Garibaldi by an unknown artist.

Garibaldi and the revolutions of 1848–9

In 1848, hearing rumours of a revolution in Italy, Garibaldi decided to return home, accompanied by 60 of his men and a number of out-of-date weapons. When he arrived in Nice, he immediately offered his military services to Charles Albert, King of Piedmont. This was a surprising thing for him, as a declared republican, to do. Charles Albert must have been surprised also. The king mistrusted the offer and refused to see Garibaldi, sending him instead to the war minister, who also refused the offer. Nobody, it seemed, trusted or wanted Garibaldi and his red-shirted devoted followers, the *Garibaldini*.

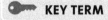 **KEY TERM**

Garibaldini The soldiers of Garibaldi, also known as legionaries and Red Shirts.

SOURCE C

> How has the image of Garibaldi in Source B been altered to produce the religious representation of the man shown in Source C? **?**

A lithograph of Garibaldi from 1850, likening him to Christ.

Garibaldi instead enlisted in the army of the revolutionary government of Milan in Lombardy, but before his men could see much action the news came that Charles Albert's Piedmontese army had been defeated at Custoza (see page 56). On hearing this, most of the legionaries deserted, and the few who remained with Garibaldi took action in only a few minor skirmishes. Later, an Austrian general remarked that the one man who could have helped Piedmont win the 1848 war was the one man they turned their backs on.

Why did Garibaldi offer his services to Charles Albert? He seems to have believed that only Charles Albert, as King of Piedmont, had the resources to defeat the Austrians and unite Italy. It was a decision that constituted a turning point in his life, as he abandoned the republican preference he had learnt from

Mazzini. 'I was a republican', Garibaldi insisted, 'but when I discovered that Charles Albert had made himself champion of Italy I swore to obey him and faithfully to follow his banner.' Mazzini was hurt at what he saw as a betrayal, and Charles Albert failed at first to welcome his new follower; but Garibaldi, always single-minded in his devotion to the cause of Italian unity, could see no way of achieving it except by attaching himself to Charles Albert and afterwards to his successor.

The Roman Republic 1849

The Roman Republic was declared in February 1849, after the Pope had refused to make political changes to the government of Rome and was forced to escape from the city to safety in southern Italy (see page 39). The Republic was short lived, surviving for only four months. It was led by a triumvirate headed by Mazzini. Some thought that, under his influence, Rome had never been better governed.

Garibaldi and the legionaries arrived in Rome as the city prepared, in Mazzini's words, 'to resist, resist whatever the cost, in the name of independence, in the name of honour and the right of all states, great or small, weak or strong, to govern themselves'.

Garibaldi appeared a striking figure, patrolling the city defences. He was described by a Dutch artist who saw him in Rome in 1849, in Source D.

? How realistic do you find the description in Source D?

SOURCE D

From a description of Garibaldi by a Dutch artist, quoted in George Macaulay Trevelyan, *Garibaldi's Defence of the Roman Republic*, Cosimo, 2008, p. 117.

Garibaldi entered through the gate. It was the first time I had seen the man whose name everyone in Rome knew and in whom many had placed their hopes. Of middle height, well built, broad shouldered, his square chest gives a sense of power – he stood there before us; his blue eyes, verging on violet, surveyed in one glance the entire group. Those eyes had something remarkable … they contrasted curiously with those dark sparkling eyes of his Italian soldiers, and his light chestnut brown hair, which fell loosely over his shoulders, contrasting with their shining black curls. His face was burnt red with the sun and his face covered with freckles.

A heavy moustache and a light blonde beard ending in two points gave a military expression to his face. Most striking was his broad nose which has caused him to be given the name of Leone and indeed made one think of a lion; a resemblance which, according to his soldiers, was still more conspicuous in a fight when his eyes shot forth flames and his hair waved as a mane upon his head.

He was dressed in a red tunic and on his head was a little black felt, sugar loaf hat, with two black ostrich feathers. In his left hand he had a sabre and a cartridge bag hung from his left shoulder.

The Pope had appealed to Austria and Spain for help, but it was not from these Catholic monarchies – which might have been expected to come to the aid of the Pope – but from the president of another republic, Louis Napoleon of France, that help came. A French army arrived at the gates of Rome, but was driven back. Then, during a temporary truce, French reinforcements arrived. The end came quickly as the defenders, heavily outnumbered, fought bravely but in vain. At the beginning of July the Roman Republic fell to the soldiers of the French Republic.

The march to the coast

On the day before, Garibaldi had made a theatrical entry into Rome's Assembly with a sword so bent and battered from hand-to-hand fighting that it would no longer fit in its scabbard. He announced that further resistance was useless. The Assembly appointed him 'dictator' of Rome to make what arrangements he thought necessary.

Garibaldi outlined the possible actions to the Assembly:

- to surrender the city (impossible)
- to continue to fight inside the city (suicidal in view of the greatly reinforced French army now numbering 20,000 men, twice the size of the defending army)
- or to withdraw as many men as possible towards Venetia, where the republic there was still holding out against a besieging Austrian army (the only acceptable option).

SOURCE E

From Garibaldi's appeal to the crowd in the Piazza of St Peter, quoted in Alfonso Scirocco, *Garibaldi: Citizen of the World*, Princeton University Press, 2007, p. 170.

Fortune who betrays us today will smile on us tomorrow. I am going out from Rome. Let those who wish to continue the war against the stranger, come with me. I offer neither pay, nor quarters, nor provisions; I offer hunger, thirst, forced marches, battles and death. Let him who loves his country in his heart, and not with his lips only, follow me.

Why do you think the crowds cheered the words in Source E? **?**

Garibaldi collected nearly 5000 men, almost all the soldiers who had not been killed in the defence of Rome, and began a forced march towards the Adriatic coast.

This march became one of the epic tales of the *Risorgimento*. Over 800 kilometres of mountainous country, a shortage of food and water, and pursuit by enemy troops all took their toll. Only 1500 men reached the coast. Garibaldi's wife Anita, who had accompanied him everywhere during the past ten years and often fought alongside him, died on the way and he was unable to stop for long enough to bury her. Many of the *Garibaldini* were killed or captured or deserted to become bandits.

Garibaldi himself escaped to Genoa, where he was arrested but later freed on condition that he left Italy at once. His career as a revolutionary soldier-hero seemed to be over, the drama played out, the legend finished as he once again set sail across the Atlantic, this time to North America.

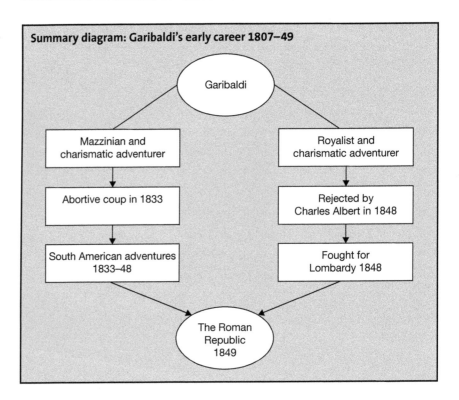

Summary diagram: Garibaldi's early career 1807–49

② Garibaldi and 'The Thousand'

▶ *What caused friction between Cavour and Garibaldi?*

▶ *How did Cavour and Garibaldi's disagreements further the cause of unification?*

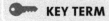

KEY TERM

National Society A body set up in 1856 by moderate republicans, aiming to bridge the gap between Mazzini and Garibaldi. Led by the Venetian Daniele Manin, it began to look to the Piedmontese monarchy to spearhead unification.

Exile and royal service 1849–59

In the USA Garibaldi found what employment he could, eventually going back to sea as master of a ship travelling between the USA and China, until he inherited some money from his brother. He used this to buy half of the small island of Caprera off the coast of the island of Sardinia. There he took up farming but was able to keep in touch with events in Italy through the **National Society**, which was working for the unification of Italy not as a republic but as a monarchy under the leadership of the King of Piedmont.

In the ten years since Garibaldi had left Italy there had been many changes. The situation in Piedmont itself was greatly altered. Charles Albert had been succeeded by his son, Victor Emmanuel, who was pleasant, easy-going and rather lazy, and not unlike Garibaldi in his down-to-earth honest approach and somewhat uncultivated manners. The king was, however, much more politically able than he appeared and managed somehow to keep on good terms with both Cavour and Garibaldi. He inspired great loyalty from the latter, though without returning it.

Cavour was by now chief minister, but his views on the need for Italian unity were still unclear.

After his meeting with Napoleon III at Plombières in July 1858 (see page 60), Cavour sent an invitation to Garibaldi through the National Society to visit Turin. There, at a meeting with Cavour and Victor Emmanuel, Garibaldi was given details of the plans for forcing war on Austria in 1859. He offered to recruit and train volunteers. Clearly, he had thrown in his lot with the Piedmontese king.

In the spring of 1859 the war against Austria began (see pages 68–70 for details of the war). The armies of Piedmont and France were badly organised, but the Austrians even more so, and French and Piedmontese troops were able to conquer Lombardy. Garibaldi, with a force of 3300 men, had performed well in the war, winning a successful Alpine campaign, but he had been kept away from the main theatre. He had effectively been sidelined because Cavour did not trust him. Even so, a successful war required heroes, and Garibaldi was presented by Victor Emmanuel with the gold medal for valour, the highest military decoration in Piedmont.

Victor Emmanuel was now king of all northern Italy except for Venetia. But as part of the agreement with Napoleon for French support during the war, Nice and Savoy had to be ceded to France; and the handing over of Nice, the city of his birth, was a bitter blow to Garibaldi. He now decided that Cavour was 'a low intriguer'. A crisis point had been reached.

The expedition to Sicily

The preparations

In April 1860 a revolt started in Palermo in Sicily against the King of Naples. It was almost certainly organised by followers of Mazzini, who urged Garibaldi to take his men to the island, and it was supported by the National Society with its contacts throughout Italy. At the time Garibaldi was preparing for an armed expedition to recover Nice from France. This would include blowing up the ballot boxes to be used by those voting on whether Nice should remain Italian or again become French. He was, fortunately for the cause of Italian unity, diverted from this plan by news of the revolt in Sicily.

Garibaldi began to collect more volunteers and by early May 1860 had a force of about 1200, mostly very young men, who were known, with numerical inaccuracy, as 'The Thousand'. He also had with him his current mistress and 1000 rifles, but no ammunition. They boarded two old paddle steamers in the port of Genoa, ready to sail in the name of 'Italy and Victor Emmanuel'. He announced that 'The mission of this corps will be based, as it always has been, on complete self-sacrifice for the preservation of the fatherland.'

Cavour's attitude

Common sense suggested to the Piedmontese prime minister, Count Cavour, that the expedition was unlikely to succeed. It had been put together too quickly, the number of men was too small and their resources too poor, while it was known that the enemy forces were large. It was also known that previous expeditions of this kind had failed, including a much larger one in 1857. Garibaldi might be a brilliant leader of men but he had no understanding of military tactics. Cavour, therefore, was far from convinced that the expedition would succeed. Nor was he sure it was a good idea. In his opinion Sicily, like the rest of the south, was too poor and backward to be ready for a takeover by Piedmont. He therefore refused Garibaldi's request for arms and equipment for the expedition, and made it clear that it went without Piedmontese official support.

Some later reports suggested that Cavour tried to persuade Victor Emmanuel to arrest Garibaldi. But it was too late. The expedition had sailed on 5 May.

In a note to his confidential agent in Paris, Cavour made it clear that he had 'made every effort to persuade Garibaldi to drop his mad scheme', but could 'not stop him going, for force would have been necessary', which would have led to 'immense unpopularity had Garibaldi been prevented'. In the end he comforted himself with the idea that if the expedition failed he would be rid of Garibaldi, 'a troublesome fellow', and if it succeeded 'Italy would get some benefit from it'.

Success in Sicily

Garibaldi reached Marsala in Sicily on 11 May. He was lucky to be allowed to land. His two steamers arrived alongside a detachment of Britain's navy, and the local commander – quite wrongly – thought Garibaldi was under British protection and so refrained from attacking, whereas in reality there was no connection at all. Garibaldi benefited from this happy accident. When the commander realised his error and did fire, most of the Red Shirts had been evacuated, so that the only casualties were a man wounded in the shoulder and a dog wounded in the leg. It was an auspicious start.

From Marsala, Garibaldi advanced on Palermo, the island's capital, gathering support on the way and defeating a Neapolitan army in hand-to-hand fighting. In pouring rain 'The Thousand' – now numbering nearer 3000 – reached

Palermo at the end of May and found 20,000 enemy troops waiting for them. The ensuing battle for Palermo is described by one of 'The Thousand' in Source F.

SOURCE F

From a description of Palermo by one of 'The Thousand', quoted in Dennis Mack Smith, *Garibaldi*, Prentice-Hall, 1969, p. 43.

*There was no sign of any local uprising until quite late in the day. We were on our own, 800 of us at most, spread out over an area as large as Milan. It was impossible to expect any planning let alone any orders, but somehow we managed to take the city against 25,000 well-armed and well-mounted regular soldiers. We were real ragamuffins … we ran in ones and twos through alleys and squares chasing Neapolitans and trying to stir up the **Palmeritans**. The Neapolitans were too busy running away and the Palmeritans in taking refuge from the gunfire … when Palermo finally fell it was all our doing, ours alone. Garibaldi showed the height of courage and we too were heroes just because we believed in what was impossible.*

How useful is Source F in explaining Garibaldi's victory in Palermo? **?**

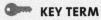 **KEY TERM**

Palmeritans Natives of Palermo.

Garibaldi quickly took possession of Palermo. The Austrian garrison withdrew to Naples and the island of Sicily was his. His success outside the capital was helped by the fact that an earlier revolt had left much of the island in a state of chaos, with bands of peasants roaming about looking for revenge against Neapolitan troops and oppressive landlords. Therefore, the speed of Garibaldi's success was partly due to his dashing and bold style of leadership and partly due to the caution of Neapolitan officers worried about possible ambushes of their men by Sicilian bandits and dispossessed peasants.

Governing Sicily

Garibaldi appointed himself as 'dictator' of Sicily and at first was sympathetic to the aims of the peasant revolt. He abolished the tax collected on corn being milled into flour, which was a standing grievance of the peasants, and won their support by promising a redistribution of land. Soon, however, he changed sides and suppressed a number of new peasant revolts. Through this he lost the support of the peasants but won that of the landlords whose help he needed to restore law and order. He needed peace and stability in the island in order to be able to use Sicily as a jumping-off ground for an attack on the mainland of Italy and the next stage of unification. His obsession with a united Italy had led him to betray Mazzini's teaching about the importance of supporting the underprivileged.

A report to Cavour on the situation in Sicily in June 1860, quoted in Source G, showed all was not well.

As part of his law-and-order campaign, Garibaldi introduced Piedmontese laws into Sicily as a preparation for annexation by Piedmont, but for the moment he refused to hand over Sicily to Victor Emmanuel. He was afraid that if he did so

? How convincing do you find the assessment in Source G?

SOURCE G

From a report to Cavour on the situation in Sicily in June 1860, quoted in Thomas Palamnenghi-Crispi, *The Memoirs of Francesco Crispi*, translated by Mary Pritchard-Agnetti, Hodder & Stoughton, 1912, pp. 247–8.

Garibaldi is greatly beloved, … but no one believes him capable of governing the State. … No one wishes to wound him, but all are determined not to tolerate a government which is the negation of all government. … Garibaldi is irritated, troubled and weary beyond belief, and his conversation plainly shows that the cares of government are crushing and overwhelming him. I have never seen him in such a state.

Cavour would stop him using Sicily as a base for the campaign against Naples. Cavour was undoubtedly surprised at Garibaldi's success in Sicily and probably displeased at the public acclaim. He judged that Garibaldi was too much in the limelight and likely to take too much of the credit for himself for uniting Italy if he was allowed to continue unchecked.

Cavour would have preferred things done more quietly, more constitutionally and with the credit going to Piedmont, Victor Emmanuel and himself.

Naples

Cavour was correct in his assumption that Garibaldi would next attempt to take Naples and then move northwards. But what could he do to prevent him? He tried to arrange a revolution in Naples in favour of Victor Emmanuel, but this failed. Then he gave orders to stop Garibaldi and his men from crossing the Straits of Messina to the mainland, but Garibaldi was too quick for him: dodging the ships sent to stop him he ferried his men across the Straits to Calabria on 22 August.

Then, although heavily outnumbered, Garibaldi fought his way north towards the city of Naples. When he heard that the King of Naples had left the city, he accepted its surrender, arriving there in advance of his troops, by train and almost alone in early September.

For the next two months Garibaldi ruled as 'dictator' over the Kingdom of Naples, unable to advance any further because the way was barred by a Neapolitan military stronghold in the north. Nevertheless, Garibaldi's plan was, as soon as possible, to move northwards, to the Papal States and then to Rome, and so complete the geographical unification of Italy. The fact that he was delayed in Naples gave Cavour time to act.

Cavour forestalls Garibaldi

As we have seen (on pages 76–7), historians are uncertain about Cavour's precise motives at this stage. But he clearly did not much like what Garibaldi had been doing in Sicily and Naples and feared that an attack on Rome, such as Garibaldi intended, would lead to difficulties, especially with France.

Napoleon III was already upset because, two months earlier on his way south, Garibaldi had landed a small force in the Papal States. That expedition fizzled out, but the warning of more to come was clear. The danger was that France and the rest of Catholic Europe would act if the Pope or the city of Rome were threatened.

Cavour was aware that many of the men who had joined Garibaldi (the *Garibaldini* now numbered about 60,000 men) were Mazzinians. This meant that they were opposed to the Church and its teachings and would be only too glad to join in an attack on Rome. They were also republicans and this posed another threat. If they won control, the whole nationalist leadership might slip away from Piedmont and Victor Emmanuel, and become again republican and revolutionary. Cavour and Victor Emmanuel must have had some doubt about whether even Garibaldi could maintain control over such a large army of irregular soldiers and enforce on them obedience to the cause he said he was supporting, that of 'Italy and Victor Emmanuel'. It was all becoming very difficult for Cavour.

Cavour's most pressing need was to stop Garibaldi from attacking Rome. The only way to do this was to send an army from Piedmont through the Papal States to meet him before he could reach the city of Rome. The Pope had no wish to see either the *Garibaldini* or official Piedmontese troops in his territory, but Cavour acted anyway. Using the excuse that the Pope was unable to deal with a threatened revolt in his territory, and with the agreement of Napoleon III, the Piedmontese army with Victor Emmanuel at its head marched through the Papal States. They defeated a papal army on the way, and any civilians resisting the invasion were shot as traitors to the cause of a united Italy.

Unification almost complete

In October the Piedmontese army reached Neapolitan territory and Garibaldi and Victor Emmanuel met on 26 October at Teano in what might have been a highly tense scene. But Garibaldi had no intention of doing other than prove himself a loyal subject. With a flourish of his broad-brimmed hat he saluted Victor Emmanuel as 'the first King of Italy' and agreed that the territory he had taken should be handed over to the king.

In the ballots that were soon held in Sicily, Naples, Umbria and the Papal Marches there was an overwhelming wish for annexation by Piedmont. Nationalist feelings were running high after all the drama of the summer, and there seemed no real alternative now that the previous rulers were no longer in place (see page 78).

On 7 November Victor Emmanuel and Garibaldi rode together in a triumphal state entry into Naples. As we see in Source H, one of the staff from the French embassy in Piedmont made pertinent comments on the king and his feelings towards his most famous subject.

How could the author of these words in Source H be sure of Victor Emmanuel's personal feelings?

SOURCE H

From the writings of a French diplomat after Victor Emmanuel and Garibaldi rode together into Naples, 1860, quoted in Denis Mack Smith, editor, *The Making of Italy, 1796–1870*, Harper & Row, 1968, pp. 332–3.

The immense popularity he [Victor Emmanuel] enjoys in the old provinces of Piedmont owes more to the monarchical sentiments of the people than to the personal qualities of the King. … Events, and above all the genius of his Prime Minister [Cavour], have raised him to the position he now occupies in Italy and Europe. If ever his name becomes famous in history, his only glory will have been 'to have allowed Italy to create herself'. … Like all mediocre men, Victor Emmanuel is jealous and quick to take umbrage [offence]. He will find it difficult to forget the manner of his triumphal entry into Naples, when, seated in Garibaldi's carriage – Garibaldi in a red shirt – he was presented to his new people by the most powerful of his subjects. … People are mistaken in crediting Victor Emmanuel with a lively liking for Garibaldi. As soldiers they probably have points of contact in their characters and tastes, which have allowed them to understand each other … at times, but the hero's familiarity is very displeasing to the King. After all, what sovereign placed in the same situation would not resent the fabulous prestige of Garibaldi's name?

On the day after the state entry into Naples, Garibaldi officially handed over all his conquests to Victor Emmanuel, who in return offered him the rank of major general, the title of prince, a large pension and even a castle. Garibaldi refused them all – 'All I want is a bag of seed corn for my farm at Caprera' – because he felt that the king had behaved badly towards the Red Shirts. He had refused to inspect them and had not signed the proclamation of thanks sent to them. Soon afterwards the *Garibaldini* were disbanded, their services no longer required. As Garibaldi said, 'They think men are like oranges; you squeeze out the last drop of juice and then you throw away the peel.'

Garibaldi retired to his island of Caprera with a year's supply of macaroni and very little else. Both Victor Emmanuel and Cavour were determined that Garibaldi should leave active political life. As far as they were concerned, his job was done. (As shown in Source I below, several key figures wished to snuff out even his reputation.) All Italy except for Rome and Venetia had been united under Victor Emmanuel and the constitution of Piedmont had been extended to the whole of the new Kingdom of Italy. If Garibaldi remained politically active, he was likely to cause trouble.

Garibaldi, however, did not agree that his work was finished. He had his eye fixed firmly on Rome as a future target.

SOURCE I

S. GIUSEPPE GARIBALDI

'The Worship of Garibaldi.' In this cartoon of 1863, Napoleon III, Pope Pius IX and Prime Minister Rattazzi of Italy try to snuff out the candles that illuminate 'Saint Giuseppe Garibaldi'.

Study Source I. Why might the French emperor, the Pope and the Italian prime minister have wanted to remove Garibaldi from the limelight, in effect to knock him off his pedestal?

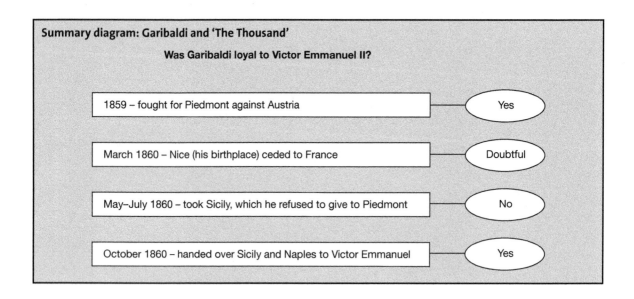

Summary diagram: Garibaldi and 'The Thousand'

Was Garibaldi loyal to Victor Emmanuel II?

1859 – fought for Piedmont against Austria	Yes
March 1860 – Nice (his birthplace) ceded to France	Doubtful
May–July 1860 – took Sicily, which he refused to give to Piedmont	No
October 1860 – handed over Sicily and Naples to Victor Emmanuel	Yes

③ Garibaldi and Rome

▶ *Why did Garibaldi twice fail to capture Rome?*

Rome was still occupied by French troops protecting the Pope, but there was continued pressure from Italian nationalists for it to be freed and included in the new Kingdom of Italy as the historical capital.

The first attempt

Garibaldi had always maintained that whenever the government found itself unable to act in the interests of national unity, it was the right of volunteers to take independent action. Thus, in 1862 he returned to Sicily from Caprera and collected together about 3000 volunteers for the conquest of Rome. Apparently with the approval of Victor Emmanuel but not of the Piedmontese government, Garibaldi set off on the march north. He did not know that Cavour's successor as prime minister, **Urbano Rattazzi**, had planned a similar coup to that of 1860. The Italian premier aimed to invade papal territory with a Piedmontese army which would reach the city of Rome before Garibaldi could. The plot failed because the French would not agree.

Garibaldi had already reached Palermo and been greeted with joyous shouts of 'Rome or Death'. Victor Emmanuel, sensing danger, immediately withdrew his support. No one tried to stop Garibaldi crossing the Straits, for the message sent to the naval commander at Messina was so vague that he ignored it and allowed Garibaldi and his men to cross to Calabria. There, in bad weather, they were shot at by local troops and forced to retreat into the mountains. All except 500 of the men deserted. Those who remained were defeated at Aspromonte in

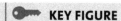
KEY FIGURE

Urbano Rattazzi (1808–73)

Born in Turin. A lawyer and politician. Supporter of Cavour and opponent of Garibaldi. Prime minister in 1862 and 1873.

a short battle with government troops at the end of August. Garibaldi, much to his annoyance, was shot in the leg and captured (see Source J below). He was imprisoned for a time and then returned to Caprera.

SOURCE J

'Garibaldi Wounded at Aspromonte.' In this nineteenth-century painting an Italian general receives the surrender of the wounded Garibaldi. Such was his fame that the bandages around his calf were later venerated by some as sacred relics.

What aspects of the painting in Source J help to explain why Garibaldi's reputation survived his failed first expedition to Rome?

The whole adventure had turned into a disaster for Garibaldi personally and militarily. He was not used to being wounded or to being defeated. The government too was embarrassed that the old hero, one of those responsible for the unification of Italy, had been defeated and imprisoned by the government of the kingdom he had done so much to create.

The second attempt

All was not quite over for Garibaldi. In 1864 the Italian government agreed to protect Rome from attack and to relocate the Italian capital from Turin in Piedmont to Florence in Tuscany, an indication that the ruling politicians no longer wanted Rome as the capital. In return the French agreed to withdraw their troops from Rome. This arrangement was not popular in Italy, however, as most Italians still wanted 'the Eternal City' as their capital. Riots in Turin left two dozen dead.

The deal was implemented eventually. In April 1865 Florence was proclaimed the capital of Italy, and in December 1866 the last French troops duly left Rome. Garibaldi now decided on action. He escaped from house arrest on Caprera and, disguised as a fisherman, sailed in a dinghy across to the mainland, where he retook command of his men. Their aim was 'to capture Rome and abolish the Pope'. He hoped that local anti-papal uprisings would take place in Rome. These did not happen, but he and his men marched towards Rome anyway. France sent an army equipped with the new, and very effective, **breech-loading rifles** back to Rome, and when Garibaldi attacked at Mentana on 3 November he was easily defeated. His second attempt to take Rome had ended in complete failure, and as a result the French were back in Rome. This marked the end of Garibaldi's part in Italian history, although not the end of his active life.

French service

In 1870, after the defeat of Napoleon III by the Prussian army and the end of the Second French Empire, Garibaldi offered his services to the new French Republic, that was, briefly, carrying on the war. 'What remains of me is at your service', he wrote to the new republican government, in typically flamboyant terms; 'dispose of me.' The French government hesitated to accept. After all, Garibaldi was now 63 years old, suffering badly with arthritis and still troubled by the wound received at Aspromonte. He did not seem the ideal choice for a military leader on active service; but, under pressure from public opinion, the French government appointed him General of the Vosges army, a hotchpotch of sharpshooters and other irregular troops, who managed under Garibaldi's leadership to defeat the Prussians in three small battles.

Afterwards Garibaldi was elected to the French National Assembly in recognition of his services, but finding his fellow members unfriendly towards him, he returned to his home on the island of Caprera where he remained until his death, at the age of 75, in 1882.

Meanwhile, French troops having been withdrawn to meet dangers from Prussia at home, Rome had been attacked and captured in 1870 by Italian troops (see page 109). Garibaldi was distressed that the government should have taken what he thought was unfair advantage of Napoleon III's misfortunes. The man who had tried so hard to take Rome felt it was wrong to do so in such inglorious circumstances.

(see page 109)

KEY TERM

Breech-loading rifles Rifles whose bullets are loaded through the chamber (or breech) rather than through the barrel (or muzzle). They could be fired four or five times more quickly than muzzle-loaders, and soldiers could load them lying down.

Summary diagram: Garibaldi and Rome

1862	Garibaldi's first attempt – defeated by Piedmontese forces
1864	Agreement between France and Piedmont
1865	Florence became Italian capital
1866	French troops left Rome
1867	Garibaldi's second attempt – defeated by French forces

Garibaldi: an assessment

▶ *Why was Garibaldi such a successful military leader and yet so unsuccessful as a politician?*

Garibaldi's contribution to the cause of Italian unity was considerable. His flamboyant personality, his striking appearance, his theatricality, his bravery, his legendary adventures both inside and outside Italy, his success with women – all these made him always the centre of attention. He represented the non-intellectual, active approach to Italian unity, a very different approach from that of Mazzini or Cavour.

As a soldier

Garibaldi was a good, sometimes brilliant, commander, excellent at sizing up the situation, decisive and determined. He and his men were best at hand-to-hand fighting, surprise night attacks and ambushes by day. He could appear authoritarian but relied more on his strong personality rather than strict discipline to keep control over his men. Regular Italian officers who visited his camp on the outskirts of Rome in 1849 were shocked by the informality.

SOURCE K

From an account by an Italian officer, quoted in George Macaulay Trevelyan, *Garibaldi's Defence of the Roman Republic*, Cosimo, 2008, p. 140.

Garibaldi and his officers were dressed in scarlet blouses with hats of every possible kind, without distinguishing marks and without any military insignia. They rode on [South] American saddles, and seemed to pride themselves on contempt for all the usual military requirements … they might be seen hurrying to and fro, now dispersing, then again collecting, active, rapid, untiring … We were surprised to see officers including the General himself leap down from their horses and attend to the wants of their own steeds … If they failed to obtain provisions from neighbouring villages, three or four colonels and majors threw themselves on the back of their horses and armed with long lassoes set off in search of sheep or oxen.

Garibaldi meanwhile … would lie stretched out under his tent made from his unrolled saddle. If the enemy were at hand he remained constantly on horseback, giving orders and visiting outposts; often, disguised as a peasant, he risked his own safety in daring reconnaissances … Garibaldi appeared more like the chief of a tribe of Indians than a General, but at the approach of danger, and in the heat of combat, his presence of mind and courage were admirable.

> What does Source K reveal about the strengths and weaknesses of Garibaldi as a military commander? **?**

Garibaldi was what we would today call a guerrilla fighter, and as a leader of a guerrilla force he was unrivalled. He inspired great enthusiasm and devotion in his men, firing them with the same passionate belief in Italian unity that he had himself – at least when there was fighting to be done. During times of inaction, or if things became bad, they showed a regrettable tendency to desert. Perhaps Garibaldi's relaxed style of leadership and the general lack of discipline made this inevitable.

It should be realised that an important factor in Garibaldi's military success was the incompetence and lack of enthusiasm shown by the enemy. In Naples in 1860 the king and his troops were so frightened by what Garibaldi had achieved in Sicily that they put up little resistance. In Sicily he had been helped by the general confusion on the island following the peasants' revolt and by local hatred of the remaining Neapolitan troops, who had an unenviable reputation for cruelty. Nevertheless, Garibaldi's conquest of the south was a remarkable achievement and a major element in the successful unification of Italy. He and his men accomplished it almost unaided in a very short time against all odds and expectations.

As a politician

Whether it was wise to unite north and south in this sudden and violent way is another matter. There was support in the south for an end to the rule by an oppressive and absolute monarch (the King of Naples), but this did not mean that there was a demand for union with Piedmont. Garibaldi and his men nearly all came from the north and had little understanding of the problems of the hot, dry south.

Much more could have been done for the peasants, particularly in Sicily. Opportunities to win popular support were missed everywhere. Perhaps if Garibaldi had not conquered southern Italy in his whirlwind campaign, the unsuitable Piedmontese legal and other systems would not have been introduced into southern Italy, certainly not so quickly.

Garibaldi was driven by his devotion to the idea of Italian unity. Everything he did was directed at achieving it. It became an obsession and as a result he could appear to lack principles. From being a republican he had suddenly became a royalist in the service first of Charles Albert and then of Victor Emmanuel; from a supporter of popular revolution he became a supporter of the establishment. In each case he was acting in what he considered to be the best interests of Italian unity. He could have ruled an independent southern Italy himself, but national unity was more important to him than personal power.

Garibaldi did, of course, have his limitations. He was not very well educated and not much of a thinker. His greatest weakness was probably his impatience for immediate action. He acted first and thought afterwards, if at all, for his actions were dominated by his heart, not his head. His understanding of politics was limited. He was not interested and was often unaware of the effect his actions might have on international relations, as in his plans to march on Rome in 1860, 1862 and 1867. Even if he had been aware of diplomatic repercussions, however, it is doubtful whether he would have been at all concerned.

That chance meeting with Mazzini in 1831 had given him his ideals and his purpose in life. Although he fell out with Mazzini, he never forgot 'Young Italy' or Mazzini's words: 'Without unity there is no true nation, without unity there is no real strength, and Italy, surrounded as she is by powerful, united and jealous nations, has need of strength above all things.' In Garibaldi Italy found much strength.

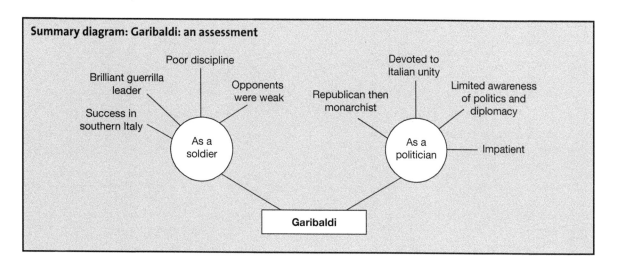

Summary diagram: Garibaldi: an assessment

Chapter summary

Many see the swashbuckling, honest, 'unpolitical' figure of Garibaldi as the true hero of the *Risorgimento*. He was certainly an adventurer, a dashing, charismatic figure and a soldier of genius. He became devoted to the unification of Italy after meeting Mazzini in 1831, and in 1848, laying aside republican principles, he agreed to serve King Charles Albert of Piedmont. It was in the defence of the Roman Republic in 1849, however, that he became an Italian hero, and as leader of 'The Thousand' in Sicily and Naples, against the wishes of Piedmont's Prime Minister Cavour, that he made his greatest contribution to Italian unification. He conquered half the peninsula and would have attacked Rome had not Piedmontese troops circumvented him.

In 1859 Garibaldi could have ruled southern Italy himself. Or, by fighting against Piedmont, he could have plunged Italy into bloody civil war. Instead, he agreed to hand over Naples and Sicily to King Victor Emmanuel II of Piedmont, thus preparing for the creation of the Kingdom of Italy. His later, unsuccessful attempts to take Rome underline the fact that the great soldier had only limited political and diplomatic skills.

Refresher questions

Use these questions to remind yourself of the key material covered in this chapter.

1 Why did Garibaldi become a figure of international renown?

2 What were the reasons for Charles Albert's refusal of help from Garibaldi in 1848?

3 In what ways did the defence of Rome and then the march to the coast enhance Garibaldi's reputation?

4 How did Garibaldi manage to conquer Sicily?

5 Did Garibaldi govern Sicily effectively?

6 Why did Garibaldi have such easy success in Naples?

7 Why was Cavour so worried about Garibaldi's progress from Sicily northwards?

8 Why did Cavour and Victor Emmanuel wish Garibaldi to play no further part in Italian affairs?

9 How can we account for Garibaldi's attempts to conquer Rome?

10 What motivated Garibaldi to work for France in 1870?

11 How good a soldier was Garibaldi?

12 In what ways was he a poor politician?

13 Was his contribution to the unification of Italy necessarily beneficial to Italians?

 Question practice

ESSAY QUESTIONS

1 'The man who contributed most to the creation of a united Italy was Giuseppe Garibaldi.' How far do you agree?

2 'Garibaldi's successes in Sicily and Naples were due more to favourable circumstances than to exceptional generalship.' How far do you agree?

3 To what extent did Garibaldi's actions produce Italian unification by 1861?

4 'Garibaldi's contribution to the unification of Italy has been exaggerated: he caused more problems than he solved.' How far do you agree with this statement?

INTERPRETATION QUESTION

1 Read the interpretation and then answer the question that follows. 'Success came in 1859–60 because Cavour had a clear and consistent aim, the unification of Italy under the Sardinian monarchy.' (From *Nationmaking in Nineteenth Century Europe*, W.G. Shreeves, 1984, p. 62.) Evaluate the strengths and limitations of this interpretation, making reference to other interpretations you have studied.

SOURCE ANALYSIS QUESTIONS

1 Why is Source 1 valuable to the historian seeking to understand relations between Cavour and Garibaldi in 1860–1? Explain your answer using the source, the information given about it and your own knowledge of the historical context.

2 How much weight do you give the evidence of Source 2 for an enquiry into the Piedmont government's hostility to Garibaldi in 1860? Explain your answer using the source, the information given about it and your own knowledge of the historical context.

3 How far could the historian make use of Sources 3 and 4 (page 106) together to evaluate the reasons for Garibaldi's successes in the unification of Italy? Explain your answer using both sources, the information you have about them and your own knowledge of the historical context.

SOURCE 1

Cavour writing to Constantino Nigra, the Piedmontese minister in Paris, 12 July 1860, quoted in Denis Mack Smith, *The Making of Italy*, Palgrave Macmillan, 1988, pp. 325–6.

Garibaldi has become intoxicated by success and by the praise showered on him all over Europe. He is planning the wildest, not to say absurdest schemes. As he remains devoted to King Victor Emmanuel, he will not help Mazzini or republicanism. But he feels it his vocation to liberate all Italy, stage by stage, before turning her over to the King. He is thus putting off the day when Sicily will demand annexation to Piedmont, for he wants to keep the dictatorial powers which will enable him to raise an army to conquer first Naples, then Rome, and in the end Venice. Some people even maintain that in private conversation he does not conceal his intention of taking Nice back from France! … The government here has no influence on him. On the contrary he mistrusts everybody whom he imagines to be in touch with us …

SOURCE 2

Garibaldi, in his memoirs, published in 1908, recalls the events of April and May 1869, quoted in Denis Mack Smith, editor, *Garibaldi: A Portrait*, Passigli Editori, 1982, pp. 30–1.

Every possible obstacle was put in our path … Some people try to argue that the government could have stopped us and yet let us go, but I deny that they could have stopped us. Public opinion was irresistibly on our side from the first moment that news spread of the Sicilian uprising in April 1860. It is true that the government put no absolute veto in our way; nevertheless they raised every kind of obstacle. I was not allowed to take any of the 15,000 muskets which belonged to our Million Rifle Fund and were kept by us in storage in Milan. This one fact delayed by several days the sailing of our expedition. La Farina [one of Cavour's ministers] then gave us 1,000 bad firearms and 8,000 lire.

SOURCE 3

From a description of Garibaldi by a Dutch artist, quoted in George Macaulay Trevelyan, *Garibaldi's Defence of the Roman Republic*, Cosimo, 2008, p. 117.

Garibaldi entered through the gate. It was the first time I had seen the man whose name everyone in Rome knew and in whom many had placed their hopes. Of middle height, well built, broad shouldered, his square chest gives a sense of power – he stood there before us; his blue eyes, verging on violet, surveyed in one glance the entire group. Those eyes had something remarkable … they contrasted curiously with those dark sparkling eyes of his Italian soldiers, and his light chestnut brown hair, which fell loosely over his shoulders, contrasting with their shining black curls. His face was burnt red with the sun and his face covered with freckles.

A heavy moustache and a light blonde beard ending in two points gave a military expression to his face. Most striking was his broad nose which has caused him to be given the name of Leone and indeed made one think of a lion; a resemblance which, according to his soldiers, was still more conspicuous in a fight when his eyes shot forth flames and his hair waved as a mane upon his head.

He was dressed in a red tunic and on his head was a little black felt, sugar loaf hat, with two black ostrich feathers. In his left hand he had a sabre and a cartridge bag hung from his left shoulder.

SOURCE 4

From Garibaldi's appeal to the crowd in the Piazza of St Peter in July 1849, quoted in Alfonso Scirocco, *Garibaldi: Citizen of the World*, Princeton University Press, 2007, p. 170.

Fortune who betrays us today will smile on us tomorrow. I am going out from Rome. Let those who wish to continue the war against the stranger, come with me. I offer neither pay, nor quarters, nor provisions; I offer hunger, thirst, forced marches, battles and death. Let him who loves his country in his heart, and not with his lips only, follow me.

CHAPTER 5

The Kingdom of Italy 1861–96

This chapter explains the events that completed the process of unification in 1870, and then considers the condition of Italy in 1861–70 and in the period after 1870. It assesses how the new Italian state functioned, examining the problems it faced, the policies it pursued, and the economic and social progress that was made. Overall, the chapter enables you to assess whether life improved for Italians, and therefore whether unification had been worthwhile. It is divided into the following sections:

★ Unification completed

★ The Kingdom of Italy 1861–70

★ Italy after 1870

Key dates

1861	March	The Kingdom of Italy was proclaimed	1870		Start of Franco-Prussian War
1861–5		Civil war (Brigands' War) in southern Italy		July	The Doctrine of Papal Infallibility
1864		The *Syllabus of Errors* published		Oct.	Rome was added to Italy and became its capital
1866	July 3	Battle of Königgrätz (Sadowa)	1876		Italy's budget was balanced
		Venetia was added to the Kingdom of Italy	1882		Triple Alliance formed
			1896		Battle of Adowa

1 Unification completed

▶ *What role did Napoleon III play in adding Venetia to the new Italian state?*

▶ *By what process was Rome added to Italy?*

In March 1861 the new Kingdom of Italy was officially proclaimed. Yet unification was not complete, for both Venetia and Rome were in the hands of foreigners. Venetia was occupied by Austria, while Rome, believed by most Italians to be their natural capital, was occupied by French troops. It was not until 1866 that Venetia was successfully won back from Austria with the help of Napoleon III of France; and, despite Garibaldi's two unsuccessful attempts in 1862 and 1867 to invade and take Rome, it was not until 1870 that the city became part of a united Italy when Napoleon III ordered his occupying troops to withdraw because they were needed to defend France against Prussia.

Venetia

In 1866 the question of Venetia came to a head. First, in April, Italy signed an alliance with Prussia, whose prime minister, Otto von Bismarck, was engaged in a struggle with Austria for control of Germany. Italy agreed that if Prussia went to war with Austria within the next few months, Italy would follow Prussia and declare war on Austria.

Secondly, Napoleon III signed a secret treaty with Bismarck in June. Not only would France remain neutral in an Austro-Prussian war, but, at the end of the conflict, France would receive Venetia if Austria were defeated. This would then be given by Napoleon to Italy as a reward for providing a **second front** in the Austro-Prussian war. Once again, Napoleon III would be the sponsor of Italian nationalism, winning the gratitude of an Italian government which, he hoped, would be compliant to French wishes. Furthermore, he would gain international prestige by his generosity in favour of a liberal cause.

Knowing now that Italy would receive Venetia if Prussia won, Napoleon – with great diplomatic skill and also total lack of principle, the two often going together – needed to make sure that the same thing would happen if Austria won. He therefore signed a secret treaty with Austria in which it was agreed that if Austria defeated Prussia, Venetia would be ceded to France and passed on by Napoleon to Italy. In return, France would remain neutral during the war.

The war of 1866

The war, known in Germany as the Seven Weeks' War and in Italy as the Third War of Independence, began on 24 June 1866. Italian confidence was high, but its army was defeated by a smaller Austrian force at the (second) battle of Custoza ten days later, largely owing to poor Italian generalship. But this was really no more than a side-show.

The decisive battle was fought on 3 July by Austria and Prussia at Königgrätz, also known as Sadowa. It was a horrific encounter. According to an eyewitness account, bombs crashed around the Prussian soldiers 'through walls of clay as if they were cardboard … Chunks of wood and big tree splinters flew around our heads.' Austrian soldiers too suffered when 4000 men set out to attack the Prussian guns, a venture from which only 1800 badly wounded men returned. Many Austrian soldiers tried to reach the safety of Königgrätz, only to be drowned in water released from the waterworks which protected the town. As before, there was inadequate provision for looking after the wounded. Injured troops were left lying for up to three days on the 115 square kilometres of the battlefield. The Prussians lost almost 2000 men, the Austrians nearer 6000.

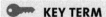

KEY TERM

Second front An alternative scene of battle, generally diverting the enemy's attention away from the major focus of a war.

The war came to an end with the Peace of Prague in August 1866. By it, Austria immediately gave up Venetia to Napoleon, who in turn surrendered it, as agreed, to Italy.

Welcome as the return of Venetia was, there was a feeling of humiliation in Italy about the way in which it had been done, not by Italians, but only as the result of action by the Great Powers of Austria, Prussia and France. At least Italians could console themselves with the thought that, once Rome was also recovered, Italian unification would be complete.

Rome

The outstanding problem now was how to get rid of the French garrison in Rome. Only then would the work of driving out the foreigners be complete. How could it be done? Again, success stemmed not from Italy's own strength but from the international situation.

In 1870 the Franco-Prussian War broke out. Conflict had been brewing between the two rival powers for some time, and in July Bismarck skilfully manoeuvred Napoleon III into declaring war on Prussia, a conflict that the Prussian leader used to whip up nationalist feeling and to unify Germany.

In an unexpected piece of good fortune for Italy, very soon after the war began Napoleon needed reinforcements to bring his army up to strength and so withdrew his troops from Rome. The Italian government made no immediate move to take over the city, but after 1 September 1870 – when Napoleon was heavily defeated at the battle of Sedan and was taken prisoner by the Prussians – they felt it safe to take action.

Victor Emmanuel, whose daughter was married to Napoleon's cousin, felt that he ought to send an army to rescue Napoleon, but his government thought otherwise. Italy had been neutral in the war and must remain so. This did not mean, though, that they could not take advantage of Napoleon's misfortunes to settle the question of Rome once and for all.

On 8 September Victor Emmanuel sent a letter to the Pope suggesting an agreement. The Pope would have to give up his temporal power, which since 1849 had depended on the support of the French troops in Rome, and allow Rome to become at last the capital of a united Italy. In return, he would be allowed to keep his spiritual power as head of the Church which would be safeguarded and guaranteed by the Italian state.

Three days later the Pope rejected this arrangement. Nevertheless, the government decided to act. An army of 6000 troops was sent to occupy Rome. Papal troops fought back briefly but the city was shelled by government artillery and a breach made in the walls. On 20 September 1870 Victor Emmanuel's army entered Rome. In October Roman citizens voted overwhelmingly (by 133,681 votes to 1507) for union with the rest of Italy, and Rome became the capital city of a politically and geographically united Italy.

Figure 5.1 The Kingdom of Italy 1859–70. Dates in brackets indicate when each state was unified with Piedmont.

Annexed to Piedmont April 1860

Ceded to France and passed to Italy by Napoleon III July 1866

N

LOMBARDY (1860)

SAVOY

TO FRANCE 1860

VENETIA (1860)

AUSTRIA

Magenta Solferino

Custozza

Turin

FRANCE PIEDMONT

TO FRANCE NICE 1860

ROMAGNA (1860)

OTTOMAN EMPIRE

PARMA (1860)

LUCCA

MODENA (1860)

TUSCANY (1860)

PAPAL STATES (1860)

KINGDOM OF SARDINIA-PIEDMONT

CORSICA (FRENCH)

Adriatic Sea

New capital of Italy 1870

Rome (1870)

Patrimony of St Peter all that was left to Pope by 1870

Naples

NAPLES (1860)

SARDINIA

0   150

km

KINGDOM OF THE TWO SICILIES (1860)

Palermo

Aspromonte

SICILY

Mediterranean Sea

Garibaldi defeated and wounded 1862

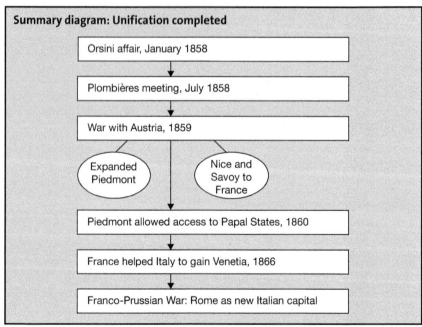

Summary diagram: Unification completed

Orsini affair, January 1858

↓

Plombières meeting, July 1858

↓

War with Austria, 1859

Expanded Piedmont

Nice and Savoy to France

↓

Piedmont allowed access to Papal States, 1860

↓

France helped Italy to gain Venetia, 1866

↓

Franco-Prussian War: Rome as new Italian capital

The Kingdom of Italy 1861–70

▶ *How did the new Kingdom of Italy function during the first decade of its existence?*

Now, in September 1870, the Kingdom of Italy seemed to be complete. The king, Victor Emmanuel II of Italy, proclaimed at the first session of the first parliament to be held in the new capital that 'The work to which we consecrated our lives is accomplished.' Yet the end of unification was only the beginning of creating a new Italy and solving the profound political, social and economic problems that were obvious to observers.

The politicians

In May 1861, with the founding of the Kingdom of Italy, Piedmont's Prime Minister Massimo d'Azeglio had remarked: 'Italy is made, now we must make Italians.' It was a pertinent remark. Yet it was far from clear that the political figures in Italy were up to the job. Certainly, the king lacked statesmanlike qualities. He was privately scornful of his new subjects, who did not seem to realise that they now belonged to the 'nation' of which he was head. 'There are only two ways of governing Italians', he half-joked, 'by bayonets and by bribery.'

Nor is it clear that the prime ministers were equal to the challenges they had to face. After Cavour's death in 1861, none of the premiers was charismatic or had the leadership qualities of the heroes of the *Risorgimento*, and most remained in power for only a short time. One prime minister, **Luigi Farini**, who suffered a mental breakdown, tried to stab the king and was removed from office after only three months, and Urbano Rattazzi (see page 89) became involved in Garibaldi's failed attacks on Rome in 1862 and 1867 and was forced to resign.

Piedmontese dominance

One major political problem was the dominance of Piedmont in the new Italy. This can be seen in several ways:

- The state was a constitutional monarchy, not the republic that Mazzini had dreamed about and worked for, nor a federation under the Pope as Gioberti and later Cavour and Napoleon III had proposed at Plombières. The constitution was based on Charles Albert's *Statuto* of 1848 (see page 54), and the Piedmontese example was closely followed. It was the King of Piedmont who became Italy's king, Victor Emmanuel II of Piedmont becoming Victor Emmanuel II of Italy – no matter that he was the *first* King of Italy. (Cavour, a typical son of Piedmont, judged that to label the king Victor Emmanuel I would 'impugn the honour of the dynasty'.)
- The Piedmontese system was extended to cover the whole country. The regional governments, for instance, were forced to accept the Piedmontese

 KEY FIGURE

Luigi Farini (1812–66)
Italian physician and politician. Minister of the interior under Cavour in 1860. Italy's fourth prime minister, from December 1862 to March 1863.

KEY TERMS

Prefects Appointees, mostly from Piedmont, who had widespread administrative powers – over law and order, local councils, press censorship and the conduct of elections – in the 60 provinces into which Italy was divided.

Legal codes Collections of laws.

Piedmontisation The forcing of the rest of Italy to adopt the laws and customs of Piedmont.

system of local administration, with local **prefects** appointed by the monarch (and later the minister of the interior), and local mayors answerable to the local prefect, rather than the electorate.

- The various **legal codes** of individual states were formed into a single criminal code based on that of Piedmont and quickly introduced everywhere except Tuscany, which kept its own moderate code. In 1865 a single system of civil law, similar to France's *Code Napoléon*, was adopted throughout the country, as it had first been in Piedmont. It allowed civil marriage, although divorce remained illegal.

- During the 1860s a unified Italian army was formed out of the old armies of Piedmont, Naples and the central Italian states, plus Garibaldi's 'Army of the South'. This was modernised and reorganised, but the majority of officers were from Piedmont. Similarly, the navies of Piedmont and Naples were amalgamated into a single force, but it was the Piedmontese who were in charge.

- Piedmont's debts, incurred during the Crimean War and the war of 1859, became Italy's debts.

- As for the electorate, the rules derived from Piedmont's constitution meant that only those who were literate and paid taxes and were over the age of 25 could vote. Around 1870 the total electorate numbered no more than 500,000 in the whole of Italy, about two per cent of the population, and the great majority of them lived in the north. It was not surprising that parliament consisted almost entirely of well-to-do traditionally minded liberals and was totally unrepresentative of the mass of the people.

Mazzini described the new state as a 'sham'. Many observers believed, with justification, that what had happened was the **Piedmontisation** rather than the unification of Italy, and that the new state had no real political maturity. One historian, writing in 1862, insisted that Piedmont 'has a thirst for power, a desire to destroy and rule … she wants to eat Italy'.

The problem of the papacy

Pope Pius IX had no reason to rejoice at the formation of Italy as a politically united state, and his policies caused grave problems for the new state.

In 1860 he had lost the majority of the land making up the Papal States (see page 72). As worldly power began to slip from his grasp, he concentrated on strengthening his spiritual power over the Church and its members. In 1864 the man who had once been thought progressive published the controversial *Syllabus of Errors*, which, turning the Church away from the material world, condemned, among other things, 'progress, liberalism and modern civilisation'. He was also against religious toleration (see Source A below). The Pope was a fundamentalist: truths were eternal and had been revealed by God to His Church; new political ideas were tantamount to heresy.

SOURCE A

The *Syllabus of Errors* issued by Pope Pius IX in 1864, quoted in Walter Kaufman, editor, *Religion from Tolstoy to Camus*, Harper & Row, 1964, pp. 162–70.

Syllabus of the principal errors of our time …

8 *All human reason is placed on a level with religion itself …*

19 *The Church is not a true and perfect society, entirely free; nor is she endowed with proper and perpetual rights of her own, conferred upon her by her Divine Founder; but it appertains to the civil power to define what are the rights of the Church, and the limits within which she may exercise those rights …*

20 *The ecclesiastical power ought not to exercise its authority without the permission and assent of the civil government …*

24 *The Church has not the power of using force, nor has she any temporal power, direct or indirect …*

73 *In force of a merely civil contract there may exist between Christians a real marriage …*

80 *The Roman Pontiff can, and ought to, reconcile himself, and come to terms with progress, liberalism and modern civilization.*

> In what ways does Source A contradict the policies of the new Italian state?

In July 1870 Pius IX went further with the Doctrine of Papal Infallibility, which decreed that the Pope's spiritual judgement on matters of faith and morals could not be challenged as he was the supreme judge of truth for the Catholic Church.

Then, three months later, Rome became the capital city of Italy and the Pope, distressed by what he called 'the triumph of disorder and the victory of wicked revolution', found himself left with only 44 hectares of land making up the area called the Patrimony of St Peter. He retired into his palace of the Vatican, describing himself as its 'prisoner'. He was offered a state pension but refused it, and instead excommunicated Victor Emmanuel and the entire Italian government.

Pius IX was determined to demonstrate his continued spiritual importance. As head of the Catholic Church, he announced that any Catholics who took part in Italian politics or worked for the new secular state would be excommunicated.

Through its beliefs, rituals and language, the Catholic Church had always been the main unifying element within Italy. Now, even though Catholicism remained the state religion, those many liberal-minded Catholics who supported the new secular government but who wished also to keep the faith found themselves in difficulties. The old balanced relationship between Church and State no longer existed. It threatened instead to become a bitter clash of personalities and values, a veritable Cold War between Church and State, as over the next two decades the Pope became ever more hostile to the Kingdom of Italy.

Economic problems

The government was faced with serious geographical, social and economic problems by the need to unite two very different areas of the country: the prosperous, semi-industrialised 'advanced' north, comprising Piedmont and her immediate neighbours, and the poor, agriculturally based 'backward' south, the regions to the south of the Papal States. Cavour had realised the enormous problems involved in uniting northern and southern Italy, claiming that 'To harmonise the north with the south is more difficult than to fight Austria or to struggle with Rome.'

The majority of the population in Naples and Sicily was illiterate, and lived in poverty and squalor, at a level of near starvation. Yet in the 1860s the new Italian government allowed the small number of great landowners in the south to enclose land to add to their estates, known as **Latifundia**, so that there was less and less land left available for the peasants. When the old **common land** disappeared into these great estates, peasant families could not feed themselves as they had done before, for they did not now have land on which to graze cattle or to grow crops.

The government also showed its total lack of understanding of the situation by introducing higher taxation, in order to help balance the budget. The cost of living rose and the quality of life for peasants fell even lower as they struggled to pay the new taxes. Their lives were further complicated by new, difficult-to-understand legal systems and, worst of all, by conscription, which took the young men away from the farms where they were needed. In 1861 around 25,000 of them took to the hills of Naples and Sicily to avoid military service. They scraped a living as bandits instead. Many in the west of Sicily joined the **Mafia** which, taking advantage of the general social unrest, was thriving, as public opinion in the south turned not just against the landowners but also against Victor Emmanuel II and Piedmont.

Peasant families began migrating to the towns in search of work and, often finding none, became part of the growing underclass of semi-destitute people whose only hope of food and shelter was to turn to crime. This was particularly the case in Palermo, the capital of Sicily, and in the overcrowded city of Naples, where the respectable citizens were 'put in fear of their lives' by half-starved beggars.

Civil war

In the early 1860s law and order, never very strong in Sicily and Naples, broke down totally. Bandits became bolder and more numerous as rural discontent fuelled a revolution which soon turned into a civil war in which more people were killed than in all the revolutions and wars of the unification period. A Piedmontese army of some 100,000 men was called in to suppress the disorder. It took them over four years, from 1861 to 1865, to do so. The government described this as the 'brigands' war', emphasising the lawlessness

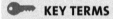

KEY TERMS

Latifundia Large estates (from the Latin *latus* meaning wide, and *fundus* meaning estate).

Common land Land held 'in common' by the people, without individual owners.

Mafia An organised criminal gang, originating as a secret society in thirteenth-century Sicily. In the nineteenth century it took this name (meaning 'swank') and virtually ruled parts of the island, sometimes protecting ordinary peasants from the oppression of corrupt police forces and judges.

of the situation and playing down the political origins of the troubles and thus their own responsibility.

Government – and of course northern – attitudes are shown clearly in an official report into the activities of a notorious southern bandit, Nunziato Mecola, as quoted in Source B. Such views justified heavy-handed retaliation not just against particular criminals but against the wider population in the south.

SOURCE B

From a government report into the bandit Nunziato Mecola who, with his supporters, entered the town of Orsonga, south-east of Rome, in January 1861, quoted in Christopher Duggan, *The Force of Destiny*, Allen Lane, 2007, p. 225.

On the morning of the 4th Mecola entered Orsonga in triumph at the head of a horde of brigands and was received by … four galantuomini [gentlemen] and the clergy carrying the statues of San Nicolò and the Virgin and preceded by a band of musicians … A hundred or so men were carrying rifles. More than two hundred were armed with pistols, knives, spits, sickles, axes, scythes and pitchforks … But what really made the blood run cold was the disorderly crowd of whorish women who were also armed and carrying sacks, an ominous and evil sign of impending pillage. After assembling in the main piazza they went into the church of San Nicolò where a solemn mass was celebrated and pictures of the Bourbon king [of Naples] and his wife were displayed …

In what ways does Source B attempt to show the complicity of large numbers of people in the activities of Mecola?

Government reactions

Government ministers made no real attempt to understand what was happening in the south. Naples, they believed, was 'rotten'. Neapolitans were 'barbarians': idle, politically corrupt and backward. They brought their troubles on themselves by their laziness, sitting about in the sun instead of working. Farini wrote of Naples: 'What barbarism! This is not Italy! This is Africa: compared to these peasants the **Bedouin** are the very flower of civilization.' Another northerner judged, in 1863, that the southerners had no sense of justice or honesty: 'In short this is a land that needs to be destroyed or at least depopulated'; he advised, ironically, that 'its inhabitants be sent to Africa to be civilized'.

 **KEY TERM**

Bedouin An Arabic word meaning 'desert-dwellers' used to refer to a group of nomadic Arab tribes.

An atrocity from one side led to retaliation from the other, and that in turn produced fresh scores that had to be settled. There was a vicious circle of violence. Government forces, usually better provisioned and armed, certainly showed no mercy. Troops were often given free rein in their attacks not only on the rebels but on the ordinary people among whom they lived or were hiding. The southerners were treated not as fellow Italians, or even as human beings, but as an inferior species.

In August 1861 General Pier Eleonoro Negri moved against the small town of Pontelandolfo, 64 kilometres north-east of Naples. Smarting from the recent loss 41 comrades, he ordered his men to shoot everyone they saw, except women, children and the infirm. The violence lasted for five or six hours.

? How would you describe the attitude of the author of Source C?

SOURCE C

The description in August 1861 by Carlo Margolfo, a conscript soldier from Lombardy, of the Italian army's raid on Pontelandolfo, where bandits had been reported, quoted in Christopher Duggan, *The Force of Destiny*, Allen Lane, 2007, p. 223.

We entered the town and immediately began shooting the priests and any men we came across. Then the soldiers started sacking, and finally we set fire to the town … What a terrible scene it was, and the heat was so great that you could not stand it there. And what a noise those poor devils made whose fate it was to die roasted under the ruins of the houses. But while the fire raged we had everything we wanted – chicken, bread, wine, capons. We were short of nothing.

The soldiers looted and pillaged at will, helping themselves to whatever of value they could find. By the time the violence ended, well over 1000 people had been made homeless, around 400 people had died, and many women and girls had been raped. The following day Negri reported to the politicians that 'At dawn yesterday justice was done to Pontelandolfo.'

At the root of the government's attitude was belief in the rightness of Cavour's original plan to reorganise the whole peninsula on the Piedmontese model, and in the idea that the south held great wealth, just waiting for the north to take and use it. On both counts they were wrong, and attempts to put them into practice only had the effect of increasing the growth of industry in the north while making matters socially and economically worse in the south. Throughout the 1860s north and south remained as far apart as ever.

The standard of living

Living standards fell throughout Italy for all social classes as the government struggled to balance the books. In the mid-1860s, when Venetia was added to the kingdom, the government's total spending exceeded its income by 60 per cent.

The level of taxation was decided not by parliament but by the king alone, and unfortunately his main interest was in making war, the most expensive activity any country can indulge in. To pay for his military activities taxes had to rise, and in 1868 the 'grist tax', an unpopular tax on grinding corn, was revived. The increased taxes fell most heavily on peasants, who could least afford to pay. Many, finding that they could not survive on the produce of their small farms, moved into the towns, as large numbers of others had done before them.

The place of women

Extensive research has been done on this topic in recent decades by Italian historians. After unification, women found themselves at first, as they had been before, second-class citizens in a macho society, both in the home, where in all social classes a wife was legally subject to her husband, and in the workplace, where working women were actively discouraged from joining the new **mutual-aid societies** which were the forerunners of trade unions. In 1862 only about 10,000 women, as opposed to about 100,000 men, were members, and women continued to be paid half as much as men for the same work and the same hours.

In the 1860s in the towns, the availability of cheap housing close to factories, which is where most of the work was available, became very important to working women. They were no longer restricted to outwork in the home or to labouring in quarries, in fields or on the roads. Until the 1870s women continued to work at home, especially once the **treadle** sewing machine came into use, but increasing numbers of women moved into the factories.

Women's work

For many women their work was making cigars, a job done exclusively by women. In one of the twenty state-owned factories, 500 workers produced 700 kilograms of cigars a day. The hours were long and the pay was low, but there was company in the rows of workers sitting side by side on high stools in the large, warm rooms. Yet there was widespread tuberculosis, caused by the overcrowded and unsanitary housing of the poor and by the fact that workers were undernourished. There was no medical treatment. It only needed one infected woman to be working in an unventilated workroom and dozens alongside her would catch the disease. Factory records show that hundreds of women on their books died from tuberculosis.

Unfortunately almost every job women turned their hands to brought them illness and deformity, whether it was making leather gloves on a cumbersome sewing machine, which meant hours of working in a cramped position; or catching a fever standing in dirty and cold stagnant water up to their waists for hours at a time soaking flax and hemp ready for spinning; or working along with their children in the newly planted rice fields of Piedmont and Lombardy, their feet and legs in muddy water from one hour after dawn until one hour before sunset as they tended the rice plants. As a result, death from malaria was common among the rice workers.

Working in hazardous conditions in the factories seemed preferable to many women. In Piedmont alone, 36,000 women worked in the silk industry in factories where their hands were ruined by boiling water in the process of reeling the silk thread off the cocoons.

The old domestic standbys of spinning and weaving came to an end when competition from the new cotton cloth imports revolutionised the textile industry. From the late 1860s onwards, cloth production moved into the factory and into the machine age, producing unexpected effects on family life.

KEY TERMS

Mutual-aid societies
Organisations formed by workers who pooled their resources to provide some financial benefits in times of hardship.

Treadle A foot-operated lever that applies power to a machine.

The family unit

Spinning and weaving in the home had previously involved the whole family, bringing together men, women and children. Factory work destroyed the family as a self-contained production unit and changed the division of labour between men and women. As a result, there was a great increase in the number of babies left at the foundling hospitals (see page 7) to free their mothers for work.

The introduction of mechanised looms in the factories eliminated the heavy work of weaving previously done by men. They found themselves no longer needed and were replaced as weavers by women and girls who were cheaper to employ, often leaving the men without work. This disturbed the long-accepted social relationships within peasant and other working families because, for the first time on any large scale, male domination was challenged as women became independent wage earners outside the home.

The majority of Italians, men as well as women, must have wondered what was so wonderful about a self-governing and united Italy, as their lot remained arduous and poverty stricken. Was this really the glorious *Risorgimento* they had heard about?

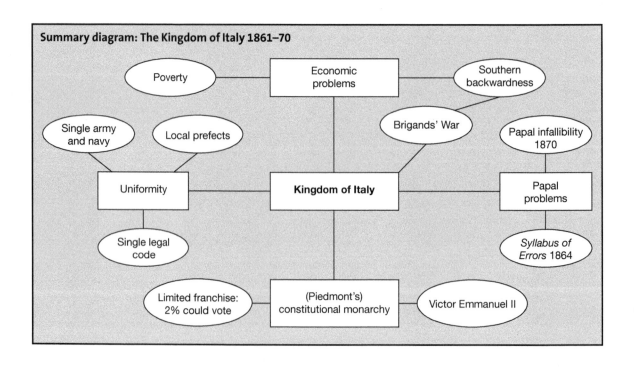

Summary diagram: The Kingdom of Italy 1861–70

Italy after 1870

> ▶ *What progress was made in solving Italy's problems after 1870?*

The first decade of existence for the Kingdom of Italy had brought profound challenges for the politicians, ones they had struggled often unsuccessfully to cope with. But a decade is a short time in the life of a nation. How fared Italy after 1870? Many of the same problems continued to exist – in particular, the challenge of how to organise the nation politically and how to overcome the stark differences between north and south. But new problems now arose, in particular how the new state would fare in an age of competitive alliances, imperialism and a struggle for dominance in Europe and the wider world.

Politics

The period after 1870 was one of profound political instability in Italy, with 29 changes in prime minister over the next 50 years. The root of the problem was the lack of a stable party system. Instead, there were competing, and shifting, interest groups or factions. Government was carried on by a system known as 'transformism' or, in Italian, *Trasformismo*. A critic of the government of the day was likely to be offered office, thus separating him from his followers and blunting the edge of opposition. To critical outsiders, this was a parliamentary game, with critics being bribed into giving their support, and one that ignored the needs of the country: it produced a form of complacent political stagnation that made for bad government. By excluding the mass of Italians from voting, the system gave the politicians no reason to attend to the wishes and needs of the mass of Italians.

Nevertheless, there are some positive things to be said about the system. The constitutional monarchy did survive, and there was no revolution. Extremists were kept out of power. Also, despite governmental instability, it allowed individuals to emerge who held power long enough to provide continuity and promote change and reform. Over the next twenty years, two men were particularly important, **Agostino Depretis** and **Francesco Crispi**.

The period dominated by these two men was marred by financial scandals, corruption and violence, but there were also important achievements and reforms, listed below:

- In 1877 free and compulsory primary education was introduced. Schools and universities came under state control as part of a policy to provide a unified system of education throughout the peninsula.
- On the death of Victor Emmanuel II in 1878, politicians ensured that his successor, Umberto IV of Piedmont, took the title Umberto I of Italy, thus giving a new, all-Italian image to the monarchy.

 KEY FIGURES

Agostino Depretis (1813–87)

A cautious and pragmatic politician, he was prime minister three times: 1876–8, 1878–81 and 1881–7, dying in office.

Francesco Crispi (1818–1901)

A much more colourful and energetic figure than Depretis. Born in Sicily, he was the first southerner to be prime minister, an office he held in 1887–91 and 1895–6.

- There was a thawing in relations with the papacy, especially after the death of Pius IX in 1878. Crispi helped to persuade the College of Cardinals to hold the conclave to choose a new Pope in Rome, thus helping to secure acceptance from Catholics for the new capital. Leo XIII, Pope from 1878 to 1903, was less of a hard-liner than his predecessor and began to see socialism as a greater threat than liberalism.
- Depretis widened the franchise in 1882, reducing the voting age from 25 to 21, so that the electorate rose from half a million to 2 million. Whereas formerly only two per cent of the population could vote, now that figure had increased to seven per cent.
- Depretis abolished the hated 'grist tax' in 1883, thereby making it easier for the poor to obtain bread.
- There were important legal reforms in Crispi's first term as prime minister, including the abolition of the death penalty and the revocation of anti-strike legislation.
- In 1889 local councils and locally elected mayors were inaugurated.
- There were public health reforms in the late 1880s.

Economic challenges

Large numbers of Italians remained in poverty after 1870 and many Italians, particularly those in the south and woman especially, suffered from malnutrition, disease and harsh working conditions. Unrest in Sicily was so bad in 1894 that Crispi sent 40,000 troops to restore law and order. Yet it remains true that there was considerable economic expansion. Statistics never tell the whole truth. In particular, they can disguise economic exploitation, and in Italy they covered up the fact that growth was much higher in the north than in the south. Yet they can give us a partial understanding of the growth in the Italian economy.

> ### Italy's economic expansion after 1870
>
> - 1873–1913: wheat production doubled.
> - Steel production: 4000 tonnes in 1880; 157,000 tonnes in 1890.
> - 1870–83: 21,000 kilometres of new roads.
> - Railways expanded from 2175 kilometres in 1870 to 8713 km in 1880 and 16,429 km in 1900.

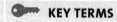 **KEY TERMS**

Land reclamation
The process of creating new, cultivable land, often by draining it of water.

Indirect taxation
Tax levied not on income but on goods or services that are bought with income.

Important irrigation improvements were made, alongside **land reclamation** schemes. There was also a good deal of mechanisation in agriculture. Perhaps the greatest achievement of the time, however, was financial, with the balancing of the budget. In 1866 the government's expenditure had exceeded its income by 60 per cent: a decade later, in 1876, the deficit had been overcome. Yet this should not disguise the fact that taxation, and particularly **indirect taxation**, was high, or that successive governments, and particularly Crispi's, were mired in financial corruption. In 1893 the Italian banking system crashed.

Foreign policy

Piedmont had achieved a considerable amount of success diplomatically and militarily in the 1850s, especially as a result of joining the Crimean War in 1855. But it had only succeeded in expelling Austria from the peninsula and unifying Italy by enlisting the military support of France. Could the new Italian state now become a Great Power, alongside the other major powers of Europe – Britain, Germany, France, Austria-Hungary and Russia? This was certainly the aim to which Italian politicians aspired. What success did they have after 1870?

This was an age of competitive nationalism and imperialism, in which many statesmen began to accept the stark alternatives that states would expand or decline, and could not simply stand still. Italy was at a disadvantage in that, although its economy was expanding, other states were industrialising more rapidly and extensively. Nevertheless, it participated in European diplomacy in an effort to win recognition of its status as a major player in international affairs and to secure its borders against possible enemies.

The Triple Alliance

Successive governments attempted to form an alliance with Germany, a state unified only in 1871 but well on its way to becoming the foremost economic and military power on the Continent. Germany's Chancellor, Otto von Bismarck, turned down Italy's request several times, but in 1882 he formed the **Triple Alliance**, between Germany, Austria-Hungary and Italy. He did not regard the alliance as particularly important, joking privately that Italy had 'a big appetite but small teeth', but to Italians it provided security against possible French aggression, and was a sign that their state was in the ascendant. In particular, Crispi now cut a figure on the European stage, meeting Bismarck several times. His rivalry with France, however, led to an unsuccessful trade war with the French in the early 1880s.

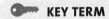

KEY TERM

Triple Alliance Under its terms, Germany and Italy would receive the other's support if attacked by France. If Austria-Hungary were at war with Russia, Italy would be neutral, thus giving Austria security on its southern border.

Imperialism

The next ambition on the Italian agenda was the acquisition of a colonial empire in Africa. Crispi was determined to achieve a new great empire. He believed that national feeling was lacking in Italy, and that Italians would only be truly united, and forget their regional affiliations, if he could generate an upsurge of patriotism in foreign policy.

At first all went well. A successful campaign in Africa was fought in the 1880s, and by the end of the decade Eritrea and Italian Somaliland had been acquired. But the attempt to conquer Ethiopia was a disaster. The campaign of 1896 led not to the expected easy victory (against a supposedly inferior race) but to a crushing defeat at the battle of Adowa. Around 7000 Italian troops were killed and 3000 taken prisoner by King Menelik and his African forces. No other European power had suffered defeat in the so-called 'Scramble for Africa', and this defeat was on a huge scale. It was a tremendous blow to Italian prestige and seemed an obvious sign of the inadequacy of the Italian state. Crispi immediately resigned and troops had to be called out to quell popular demonstrations throughout Italy.

Conclusion

A mixed record

To many, defeat at Adowa in 1896 symbolised the failure of Italian governments since the formation of the Italian state. The new *Italia* had seen political corruption and financial scandals; poverty, malnutrition and exploitations; stark differences between north and south; the dominance of Piedmont over all other regions; and a whole series of failures for which there were no compensating successes.

Yet such a view, while understandable as an emotional reaction to an unprecedented military defeat, is of course clearly biased. The judgement was fed by later critics, from ideologies on the far left and far right. Marxist critics believed that only a workers' government could bring salvation to Italy. This was the message of, for instance, **Antonio Gramsci**, who condemned the whole regime as illegitimate, undemocratic, reactionary, impotent and self-seeking. From the opposite end of the political spectrum, fascist writers also criticised liberal Italy in extreme terms, pointing to the need for a new leader of energy, dynamism and vision to restore the nation's fortunes after the rule of inadequate democrats. In short, such writers were propagandists for the fascist regime of **Benito Mussolini**.

Governments in charge of Italy from 1861 to 1896 clearly had successes and failures to their credit. The successes stemmed from the survival of the regime and reforms that improved the quality of administration, law and education in Italy, as well as involving more people in national life, and improving the standard of living. The failures stemmed from the structural problems that beset the Italian economy – and in particular the stark differences between north and south – but also from political corruption and policies that clearly failed, most importantly the disastrous Ethiopian war.

Perspectives

What is clear is that our overall assessment of the unification of Italy must depend, in part, on the record of the first Italian governments. The significance of an event is always partly determined by its effects. Were the high hopes raised by the *Risorgimento* fulfilled in the period from 1861 to 1896? This is an issue to grapple with – and most thoughtful people's answer will be neither a categorical yes or no but will lie somewhere in the middle, assigning different elements of success and failure to particular aspects of Italian history over this period.

Yet to take the story up until only 1896 is arbitrary. Why stop there, at the date of a particularly disastrous failure for liberal Italy? If we examine the period

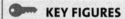

KEY FIGURES

Antonio Gramsci (1891–1937)

The founder of the Italian Communist Party in 1921 and a Marxist theorist.

Benito Mussolini (1883–1945)

He came to power as prime minister in 1922 and soon achieved dictatorial power. He avenged Adowa by conquering Ethiopia in 1935–6 but led Italy to defeat in the Second World War.

from 1896 to 1914, we are provided with more ammunition with which to judge the regime. This was a period of rapid industrial growth, with **gross domestic product (GDP) per capita** growing faster in Italy (at 2.1 per cent) than in Britain (0.9), Germany (1.8) or France (2.0). There was also a definite thaw in relations between Church and State and many state-sponsored reforms that affected Italian society. But there were continued economic problems, made more manageable by a massive emigration of Italians abroad.

Or should we take the story even further? How far is Italy's performance in the First World War a reflection of the unification of Italy? What does the collapse of democracy in Italy, and the triumph of fascism, tell us about the *Risorgimento*? How far is today's twenty-first-century debate about whether Italy should become a federal state a reflection on the unification of Italy, and the creation of a unitary state, in the nineteenth century?

The significance of the past is always dependent on future developments, but of course the further away we get from an event the harder it is to trace its effects because new factors come into play. Did Mussolini come to power, for instance, because unification was little more than Piedmontisation and created a regime that was unpopular with the mass of Italians? Or, on the contrary, did the hardships of the First World War and the rise of communism do much more to create Italian fascism? All we can say for certain is that the unification of Italy was a vitally important event, one that is embedded into the fabric of subsequent Italian history.

KEY TERM

Gross domestic product (GDP) per capita The total production, in terms of goods and services, that each person in a society is responsible for.

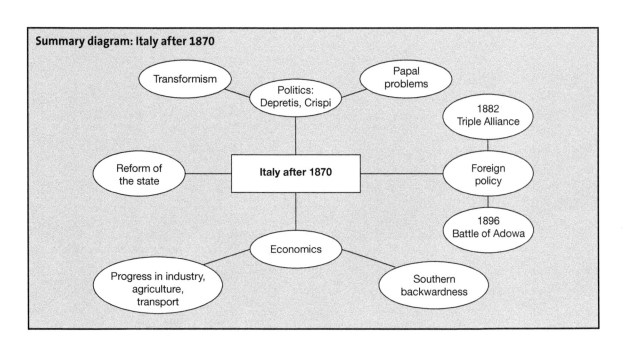

Summary diagram: Italy after 1870

Chapter summary

The creation of the Kingdom of Italy in 1861 was not the end of the unification process. In 1866, owing to Napoleon III's intrigues, war between Prussia and Austria resulted in Venetia being added to Italy. Then, in 1870, France fought Prussia and had to remove its troops from Rome, which was then taken over by Italian forces and became the Italian capital.

The new Italian state was in many ways an expanded Piedmont: its king and constitution, its voting system, its laws and local government were extended to the whole peninsula. Much of the south of the country remained economically backward and its population did not feel members of the new Italian state. Indeed, there was civil war in the south in 1861–5. Important reforms were passed, especially after 1871, so that for instance education was improved and the franchise extended, but progress was marred by financial scandals and a political system that lacked a party system and saw frequent ministerial changes. In 1896 Italy suffered a catastrophic military defeat in north-east Africa, but in fact the record of the regime is mixed, and contains successes as well as failures.

 Refresher questions

Use these questions to remind yourself of the key material covered in this chapter.

1 What was the process by which the Austro-Prussian War of 1866 led to Venetia being added to the Kingdom of Italy?

2 How did the Franco-Prussian War of 1870–1 enable Italian troops to take Rome?

3 In what ways was Piedmont dominant in the new Italian state?

4 How far did the rest of Italy have to conform to Piedmontese laws and customs?

5 What problems did the *Syllabus of Errors* and the Doctrine of Papal Infallibility pose for the Italian government?

6 Why did the system of agriculture in southern Italy produce poverty?

7 Why was there civil war in Naples and Sicily in the first half of the 1860s?

8 In what ways did the position of women in Italian society change?

9 Why was 'transformism' important in Italian politics?

10 What constructive reforms were instituted in Italy after 1871?

11 Was significant economic progress made after 1871?

12 Why was defeat at Adowa so shocking to Italians?

Question practice

ESSAY QUESTIONS

1 'The Kingdom of Italy dealt inadequately with the problems that it faced in the period 1861–96.' How far do you agree?

2 Which of the following was the greater problem for the leaders of the Kingdom of Italy after 1861?
i) Economic problems. ii) Italy's relations with other European powers. Explain your answer with reference to both i) and ii).

3 To what extent was Italy a unified nation by 1870?

4 'The Italy of 1870 was a profound disappointment to Italian nationalists.' How far do you agree with this statement?

SOURCE ANALYSIS QUESTIONS

1 Why is Source A (page 113) valuable to the historian for an enquiry into relations between the Church and the Kingdom of Italy in 1861–70? Explain your answer using the source, the information given about it and your own knowledge of the historical context.

2 How much weight do you give the evidence of Source B (page 115) for an enquiry into the government's policy of suppressing banditry in southern Italy in the 1860s? Explain your answer using the source, the information given about it and your own knowledge of the historical context.

3 How far could the historian make use of Sources B (page 115) and C (page 116) together to investigate why the so-called Brigands' War of 1861–5 took place? Explain your answer using the sources, the information given about them and your own knowledge of the historical context.

CHAPTER 6

Conclusion: the *Risorgimento* and Italian unification

This final chapter provides you with an opportunity to reflect on the content of the book as a whole and to review the process of unification. By the end of the chapter you should be in a position to make up your own mind on the key issues, particularly on how important the *Risorgimento* was in the unification of Italy, and on what combination of factors actually led to unification.

The chapter examines:

★ Mazzini's view of the Kingdom of Italy

★ The 'heroes' of the *Risorgimento*

The key debate on *page 128* of this chapter asks the question: In what sense, if any, does the concept of the *Risorgimento* explain the unification of Italy?

 1 ## Mazzini's view of the Kingdom of Italy

▶ *Why was Mazzini so critical of the new Italian state?*

In 1871 Mazzini, now 66 years old, the man who had hoped for so long for a free and united Italy, criticised the ten-year-old Kingdom of Italy in outspoken terms (see Source A).

SOURCE A

? Are the criticisms in Source A valid?

From a letter written by Giuseppe Mazzini to his friend Giuseppe Ferretti, August 1871, quoted in Giuseppe Mazzini, *Scritti Editi ed Inediti*, Cooperativa tipografico-editrice P. Galeati, 1941.

The Italy which we represent today, like it or not, is a living lie … the dead corpse of Italy.

Italy was put together just as though it were a piece of lifeless mosaic, and the battles which made this mosaic were fought by foreign rulers who should have been loathed as our common enemies. Lombardy, scene of the great Five Days in 1848, allowed herself to be joined to Italy by a French despot. The Venetians, despite their heroic defence in 1849, come to us by kind permission of a German monarch. The best of us once fought against France for possession of Rome … Southern Italy was won by volunteers and a real movement of the people, but then it resigned its early promise and gave in to a government which still refuses to give Italy a new national constitution.

The battles fought by Italy in this process were defeats … Italians are now without a new constitution that could express their will. We can therefore have no real national existence or international policy of our own. In domestic politics … we are governed by a few rich men … Ordinary people are disillusioned. They had watched … as Italy, once ruler of the civilised world, began to rise again; but now they turn away their eyes and say to themselves: 'this is just the ghost of Italy'.

Mazzini's motives

Why was Mazzini so critical of the new kingdom? Perhaps he was simply resentful of the fact that, as a still suspect revolutionary republican, he was not allowed to take the seat in parliament to which he had been elected. Perhaps he was out of touch, living emotionally in the 1840s. After all, some of his hopes had been fulfilled (the Austrians had gone, Lombardy and Venetia were back in Italian hands and Rome had become the capital city), even though not in the manner he had wanted.

Yet there was also justice in Mazzini's comments. What disappointed him was partly the way Italy had been united. Italy had not 'made herself' as he and others had hoped, but had needed foreign help. In a sense, therefore, 'Italy' had been unified prematurely, before a common struggle had first created 'Italians'. He was also highly critical of the present state of the country. Italy was free and the states were united politically but they were not united socially or economically. The division between the prosperous north and the impoverished south had not been resolved. Also, Italy was a monarchy, not a republic and, although the kingdom was a secular one, Italian life was still overshadowed by the spiritual, if not the temporal, power of the Catholic Church.

Mazzini argued that Italians had had no opportunity to create a new constitution and a new lifestyle. The strong political position of Piedmont in 1860 had enabled Cavour and his successors to force Piedmont's king and constitution on the rest of Italy, along with a liberal government. Mazzini did not quarrel with the exclusion of women as voters or candidates for election: he believed that they should stay quietly at home as daughters, wives and mothers to men and have no political or public role. But he was concerned that most of the male population, by not being allowed to vote or to stand as candidates, had been excluded from decision-making and had therefore no good reason to support the new state.

True democracy (rule by the people), which Mazzini had promised members of 'Young Italy', was as far away as ever. In his view, the spirit of the *Risorgimento* was dead, killed by Piedmont's politicians. Mazzini died in 1872, but it is easy to believe that, had he been writing as late as 1896, his fundamental criticisms would have been the same, for still Italy was not a true democracy, Piedmont's institutions were still dominant, the Church was still powerful, there were still gross economic differences between north and south, and Italy's international policy seemed to consist of aping – not very successfully – the imperialism of other European states.

Mazzini's criticisms have created much controversy among historians.

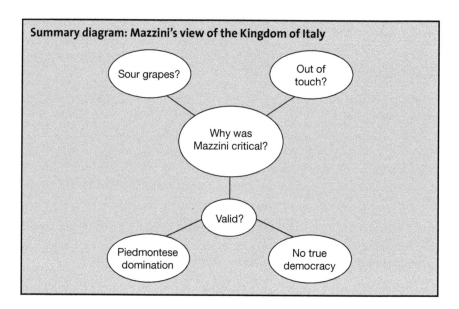

Summary diagram: Mazzini's view of the Kingdom of Italy

② Key debate

▶ *In what sense, if any, does the concept of the* Risorgimento *explain the unification of Italy?*

Both Italian and non-Italian historians have over the years developed theories about the importance or otherwise of the *Risorgimento* and have tried to define exactly what it was. While some historians see it as the mainspring of the unification movement, others have questioned whether it was ever an actual movement or only a nineteenth-century myth created by the ruling elite to justify, and thus maintain, their domination.

Italian and British views

Italian interpretations

In Italy, the belief in the *Risorgimento* as a revolutionary movement has tended to be strong. The term has often been defined as active 'resurgence' or 'national rebirth' driven by nationalist ideals of unity and independence, based on a national memory of past glory and the hope of an equally glorious future. The unification of Italy was thus heroic and magnificent.

Until recently, most Italians continued to see the *Risorgimento* as a movement in which Italy found itself as the result of a long campaign dominated by the larger-than-life patriotic leaders: Cavour, Garibaldi, Victor Emmanuel II and Mazzini. It is believed that these men acting together, with the aid of Napoleon III of France, gave Italy unity and independence. Rivalries between the heroes of the *Risorgimento* are played down as no more than temporary squabbles resulting from war, and as such they do nothing to alter the fact that the events of 1860–1 were the great romantic climax to a long process of national development and growth which gave Italy back its soul.

One problem here is that many Italian historians have also been **philosophers**, making use of rather abstruse theories and abstract ideas in their writings. Not for them the usual bread-and-butter of historians: concrete facts about nationalist movements, wars, revolutions, accidents and individuals. As a result, much of their historical writing is extremely hard to follow.

Yet it is not difficult to spot national bias, even if it is expressed incoherently and emotionally. One moderate Italian historian, writing in 1943, described the *Risorgimento* as 'a fact or better a process of a spiritual character, an intimate and thorough transformation of national life … Italy and the *Risorgimento* have both been understood over the centuries, before all else, as facts of consciousness, as spiritual attitudes.' Another Italian historian, writing in 1960, insisted 'the *Risorgimento* was not due to fortunate circumstances or to selfish interests … it was a spirit of sacrifice, it was suffering in the way of exile and in the galleys, it was the blood of Italian youth on the battlefields … it was the passion of a people for its Italian identity.' As **rhetoric**, such statements may be inspiring; as history, they may well be dismissed as inadequate.

More recently, Italians have focused not on politics but on culture. In the early years of this century Alberto Banti, of the University of Pisa, published *La Nazione del Risorgimento* (*The Nation of the Risorgimento*) and *Il Risorgimento Italiano* (*The Italian Risorgimento*). In these works, neither of which has been translated into English, he examines the creation and the dissemination of the idea of an Italian nation in art, literature and music. Looked at from this perspective, the *Risorgimento* has been revived as a key theme of late-eighteenth-century and nineteenth-century Italian history. It has also been shown that these ideas affected political associations and Italian nationalists. This new work is clearly important, but only up to a point.

Banti and others show that the *Risorgimento* undoubtedly helped to form the cultural, artistic and intellectual **milieu** in which unification was achieved. It is doubtful, however, whether their approach does more than establish that the *Risorgimento* formed a springboard from which unification arose. It may indeed have been a **precondition** for unification. Yet this new school of thought among Italian historians fails to bridge the gap between culture and the actual process of unification, which involved wars, political ambitions, betrayals and accidents.

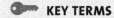 **KEY TERMS**

Philosophers Those who study the nature of reality by using logic and abstract theories.

Rhetoric Fine-sounding, but often exaggerated, language designed to affect the emotions.

Milieu A French term, meaning the total social environment.

Precondition Something without which an event could not have taken place: a 'necessary' factor but not one that is 'sufficient' on its own to explain an event.

The events of unification are in fact ignored in their work. Therefore, the new Italian approach fails to provide anything like a full explanation.

British interpretations

Non-Italian historians are much more doubtful about how far, if at all, the *Risorgimento* was important in unifying Italy. They are even more doubtful about whether the 'heroes of the *Risorgimento*' acted together to unite Italy and to give it independence. Ever since G.M. Trevelyan, writing about the *Risorgimento* in the early years of the twentieth century, suggested that it was personal hostility and not united action that motivated the 'heroes' and provided 'the mainsprings of action which created a unified state', other British historians have tended to follow a similar line. In particular, Denis Mack Smith, probably the best known British historian writing about the *Risorgimento* (1968 and 1979), has argued with an impressive level of detail that it was not the agreements but the disagreements between Cavour and Garibaldi that brought about the unification of Italy by Piedmont. Cavour united Italy not so much because he intended to or because he thought it right to do so, but because Garibaldi's unauthorised military successes in southern Italy forced him into action.

There is also a fundamental difference of approach. British historians have tended to be more down to earth and less theoretical than Italians, drawing their interpretations from a consideration of what actually happened, and therefore their writings are easier to follow. Mack Smith, for instance, is practical in that he focuses on Piedmont.

Mack Smith has argued that it was the war of 1859 against Austria in the north, masterminded by Cavour and Napoleon III, along with Garibaldi's military successes in the south and Cavour's move to stop him reaching Rome in 1860, that made it possible for Piedmont to force unification on the rest of Italy. It was not therefore the result of some intangible 'national rebirth' or *Risorgimento*. Yet it was at this point that misleading official propaganda made the *Risorgimento* a part of Italy's shared past, a myth that transformed unification into a popular quest for national freedom and unity, rather than the result of rivalry and Piedmontese expansion.

Revisionist historians point out that national unity was only one possible result of the Italian struggle for independence. It was not inevitable. They believe that it came about because of French politics and Piedmontese policies, and not from popular nationalist pressure for a unified Italy. This may well be so.

Lucy Riall has recently given a **trenchant**, and very British, interpretation (see Source B).

One might judge that, if Riall's interpretation is correct, then the idea that the glorious *Risorgimento* led to unification is totally misleading.

KEY TERM

Trenchant Expressed in strong and vigorous language.

SOURCE B

From Lucy Riall, *Risorgimento*, Palgrave Macmillan, 2009, p. 35.

The years of the Risorgimento, *and the events of Italian unification, are among the most **mythologised** in modern history, and they are also politically controversial. Behind the myth and the controversies lies the ambivalent nature of what happened in 1859–60. Garibaldi's greatest success ended in his own defeat; and the Union of North and South took place in an atmosphere of distrust, disappointment and popular disorder …*

The main architects of unity, the Piedmontese liberals, had no interest in the edifice. Those who had fought long and hard for its construction – Mazzini, Garibaldi, the democratic movement as a whole – had little part in the final result. The sense of difference and decline relative to European neighbours, which had driven successive attempts at reform and revolution in Italy since the mid-eighteenth century, was not reversed by the wars of 1859–60 with their dependence on France … The position of the people … was not altered by unification. Nor, for the most part, did the poor want or welcome these events …

What criticisms might you make of the interpretation in Source B?

 **KEY TERM**

Mythologised Exaggerated and idealised, so that it loses touch with reality.

Conclusion

Diplomacy, war and the rivalries between Cavour and Garibaldi were obviously vital factors in the unification of Italy. Nevertheless, the romantic pull of the *Risorgimento* persists and seems likely to continue to do so. Its ideals were important because they provided an emotional and political appeal, giving at least some Italians a common identity and purpose which fuelled the nationalist cause both before and after unification.

Italy was not unified solely by wars and the intrigues and rivalries of politicians. Nationalism played a part. National feeling did rouse a section of public opinion to support Piedmont's ambitions to lead a unified Italy and provide its first king and its first national constitution. Without nationalist support a united Italy as early as 1861 would not have been possible. Mazzini may have been very critical of the unification process, with its French intervention and Piedmontisation, but he himself embodied nationalist ideals. Insofar as he was important, the ideals of the *Risorgimento* were not a myth.

The 'heroes' of the *Risorgimento*

▶ *What roles should be assigned to the leading individuals – and to Piedmont – involved with Italian unification?*

▶ *Why was Piedmont so dominant in the movement for unification?*

Individuals were not all-important, but they were certainly crucial, in the unification of Italy. Four Italian 'heroes' are often singled out: Cavour, Garibaldi, Victor Emmanuel and Mazzini. Yet there was also a non-Italian, the French emperor, Napoleon III, who cannot be left out of the reckoning. What conclusions can be reached about the roles of these men?

Cavour and Garibaldi

There was indeed, as Trevelyan, Mack Smith and others suggest, hostility between Cavour and Garibaldi. How important was it? If Cavour had not distrusted Garibaldi and feared in 1860 that, after his military successes in Naples and Sicily, he might take Rome and also make himself permanent ruler of an independent southern Italy and even turn it into a republic, he would not have made the decision to invade the Papal States to prevent Garibaldi from moving against Rome. This decision led to an open quarrel between the liberal Cavour and the radical Garibaldi on the future of the Italian peninsula. It has been said, with some reason, that Cavour united Italy in order to get the better of Garibaldi, whom he still suspected of being a supporter of Mazzini.

Garibaldi, for his part, disliked Cavour personally and distrusted diplomacy. He still believed that Italy could only be united by revolutionary means, and that armed action was essential. Like the proverbial bull in a china shop, he had charged into an attack on Sicily and then Naples. After his unexpected successes there, he planned to go on to take Venetia and Rome, without considering what the results of this might be. Such action would have brought armed intervention by France to protect its garrison in Rome and probably by Austria to retain its hold on Venetia. Could the new and fragile Kingdom of Italy have withstood such a double attack? It seems unlikely.

It was Cavour's greatest contribution to unification that his invasion of the Papal States effectively prevented Garibaldi from carrying out the second part of his plan, beginning with the attack on Rome, just as it was Garibaldi's greatest contribution that he was able to carry out the first part, the conquest of Naples and Sicily, despite Cavour's opposition.

Garibaldi's willingness to surrender Naples and Sicily to Victor Emmanuel II avoided civil war and left the way clear for Cavour and Piedmont to take over Italy. Was this the act of a great and generous man laying the spoils of war at the feet of his king? Many have thought so, and British historian A.J.P. Taylor has gone so far as to describe Garibaldi as 'the most wholly admirable man in modern history' (1959). Or, on the contrary, was it merely a way of getting out of a difficult situation, now that the fighting was over? Opinion is divided on this. Yet it seems certain that Victor Emmanuel and Cavour were determined that Garibaldi's contribution was finished and that he should now quit Italian affairs, leaving them to continue in a more diplomatic way the process of unification. With no immediate prospect of further fighting Garibaldi too seems to have been quite happy to return to the simple life on the island of Caprera.

Victor Emmanuel II

How important a role did the 'gallant king' (*Il Re galantuomo*), the first king of a united Italy, play in the unification of his new kingdom? Famous for his incredibly long and deeply cherished moustaches, he was personally popular, with his bluff and hearty manner. But of his politics it was not easy to be sure.

Despite the king's frequently coarse language, Queen Victoria, in whose honour he sacrificed ten centimetres from his moustache, found him more attractive than she expected when he visited London in 1855: 'He is so frank, open, just, straightforward, liberal and tolerant, with much sound good sense.' Yet this was not the judgement of the French ambassador three years earlier. 'King Victor Emmanuel is in no sense liberal.' he wrote; 'his tastes, his education and his whole habit of behaviour all go the other way … Nor does he like parliamentary liberties, nor a free press. He just accepts them temporarily as a kind of weapon of war.'

In popular Italian mythology, Victor Emmanuel was of vital importance. The enormous Victor Emanuel Monument in Rome (see Source C, page 134) embodies such a view. Yet foreign historians have been less enthusiastic, being inclined to believe that the king's only real claim to fame is that he happened to be there at the right time to become the figurehead for Italian nationalists and, after unification, for the new Kingdom of Italy. Even Garibaldi called him merely 'the symbol of our resurgence and of the prosperity of our country'. It may have been what he represented, rather than what he did, that gave Victor Emmanuel II a special place in Italian history. Had he not been lucky when it was generally believed, probably falsely, that he alone had defied the Austrians and maintained the constitution in 1849 (see page 57)?

Although Victor Emmanuel's role was a subordinate one, he played an important part in unification. After all:

- it was he who appointed Cavour as prime minister in the first place
- he was keener than Cavour on joining the Crimean War
- he refused Cavour's unrealistic demand to carry on the war against Austria in 1859 after the French signed the armistice at Villafranca (see page 72)
- he allowed Cavour's return early in the following year
- he maintained good relations with Garibaldi and, against Cavour's wishes, he gave some encouragement to Garibaldi in 1860.

? In what ways does the monument in Source C embody the *Risorgimento*?

SOURCE C

The Victor Emmanuel Monument, in the centre of Rome, built between 1885 and 1911. Many Romans found it splendid, but others thought it vulgar and called it 'the wedding cake'.

Mazzini

Mazzini undoubtedly deserves his place in the list of 'heroes' but, unlike the others, his active contribution to Italian unification had finished long before 1861. He was the intellectual heart and mind of the nationalist movement. His great moments were in the 1830s and 1840s, when his drive for independence and unity were focused through 'Young Italy' and when, for a short time, he headed the Roman Republic.

Mazzini's reputation made him too extreme, too revolutionary and, above all, too republican and anti-Catholic to be acceptable to Piedmontese liberals or to the Church, although he was not without religious beliefs, declaring, for instance, that God spoke, not through priests because Christianity was now outmoded, but through the people. In exile he kept in touch with what was happening in Italy through the National Society, returning occasionally in secret for short visits, but after 1849 his influence steadily waned. Even so, it was he who suggested that Garibaldi take Sicily, several months before he agreed to do so. (Garibaldi, Mazzini judged, had 'a heart of gold but the brains of an ox'.) Also, he was optimistic and flexible enough in March 1860 to endorse Victor Emmanuel as Italy's leader, since that seemed to be the popular choice.

Mazzini was more popular abroad than in Italy, due largely to Piedmontese propaganda at home which painted him as far more inflexible, dogmatic and violent than was really the case. His voluminous writings in exile – some 10,000 letters and articles – were more often read by foreigners than Italians, and sometimes their tone was mystical and their meaning unclear. But to his admirers, including his biographer, Mack Smith, he was a profound political thinker. It is certainly arguable that an Italy united by Mazzinians, if indeed that was a possibility, would have been a far more just and equal society than that which actually came about after 1860.

Napoleon III of France

Napoleon III worried a great deal about what later generations would think of him, and in France historians are still divided in their opinions of his aims, ambitions and character, not surprisingly in view of his passion for secrecy and intrigue.

Napoleon's intentions

Napoleon III's motives for involving himself in Italy are hard to fathom. But whatever they were, it can be argued persuasively that without him and his army the Austrians would not have been driven out of Lombardy in 1859. Piedmont alone could not have done it. Certainly nothing in their military record, including the two battles of Custoza, suggests that Piedmontese forces were likely to succeed unaided against Austria. An independent and united Italy would surely have been impossible for many years longer.

Many Italians agreed with Garibaldi after the Peace of Villafranca: 'Do not forget the gratitude we owe to Napoleon III and the French army, so many of whose valiant sons have been killed or maimed for the cause of Italy.' Later, after the handing over to the French of Nice, Garibaldi's home town, he was less enthusiastic about Napoleon, whom he called 'a **vulpine knave**'. This should not lead us to underestimate the debt that Cavour and Garibaldi owed to Louis Napoleon, but neither should we overestimate it.

Napoleon's record

In an earlier period, Napoleon did very little to help the Italian cause; in fact, quite the opposite. In 1849 he had sent the French army to crush the Roman Republic, remaining afterwards to garrison the city and protect the Pope. At the secret meeting with Cavour at Plombières in July 1858 Napoleon's aim seems to have been not to unite Italy but, rather, to keep it divided into a federation of comparatively powerless separate states. As the war of 1859 began Napoleon proclaimed that his aim was not conquest but 'to restore Italy to the Italians'. He came, he said, in the guise of a liberator as he took command of the Franco-Piedmontese army, but unlike Napoleon I he was no military genius. After the two bloody battles of Magenta and Solferino an armistice was agreed at Villafranca in July as a result of which Austria surrendered Lombardy, via France, to Piedmont but kept Venetia. The war over, Napoleon returned to France. There he found himself the subject of criticism for his conduct of the war.

The French were not the only critics. Victor Emmanuel II and Cavour felt that Napoleon had betrayed them by going home before he had done what he promised, which was to 'free Italy to the shores of the Adriatic'; in other words, to drive the Austrians out of Venetia as well as Lombardy. Napoleon made some amends in 1866 when, as a result of his complicated diplomacy, he came into possession of Venetia and quickly handed it over to the Kingdom of Italy. But his troops only finally left Rome when he was forced to withdraw them because of France's war with Prussia in 1870.

So who did unite Italy? Cavour, Garibaldi, Victor Emmanuel II, Mazzini or Napoleon III? Was it one of them? Or some of them? Or all of them?

Piedmont

Perhaps only individual people can be heroes. But the state of Piedmont was so important in the story of Italy that we must focus briefly on its leading role.

The new united Italy became a secular constitutional monarchy rather than a republic or federation of states largely because Piedmont itself had remained politically stable as a constitutional monarchy after the failure of the 1848 revolutions. During the 1850s Piedmontese power grew. It developed:

- a strong central government
- a well-organised civil service
- an effective army, unlike any of the other states.

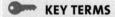

KEY TERMS

Vulpine Like a fox – cunning or sly.

Knave A scoundrel.

In addition, it forged ahead economically, partly owing to the enlightened trade and other policies pursued by its governments. Furthermore, it had as its sons not only Victor Emmanuel II but political and military leaders, including Cavour (born in Turin) and Garibaldi (born in Nice, which became part of Piedmont in 1815), who could use diplomacy and war to best advantage.

As a power

Piedmont had also acquired a sufficiently good reputation outside Italy to be able to negotiate on a nearly equal footing with the Great Powers. This reputation had been earned by the decision of the king and prime minister to support French and British forces during the Crimean War. ('I am certain that the laurels which our soldiers will win on the battlefields of the east', said Cavour, justifying his decision in the Piedmontese parliament, 'will do more for the future of Italy than all those who have sought to regenerate her with the voice and with the pen.') Piedmont had no direct interest in the war, but participation won Cavour a seat among the Great Powers at the Paris Peace Conference in 1856, and brought him into contact with Napoleon III.

As well as acquiring international influence, Cavour was finding unexpected support within Italy. The Mazzinian National Society, which had been a republican and revolutionary movement, turned its back on its origins in 1858 and began campaigning instead, in a rather limited way, for Piedmont, arguing that all Italians should rally round Cavour and Victor Emmanuel II as long as Piedmont was ready to work wholeheartedly with the Italian people and to put Italian independence and unity first.

Piedmont the model

To many it seemed natural that, since Piedmontese leaders had played such a major role in the actual process of unification, the new Kingdom of Italy should be modelled on the Kingdom of Piedmont. Those who were uncertain of Piedmont's glorious role might be convinced by the published versions of Cavour's letters, carefully edited and sometimes fabricated in the 1860s, to show Piedmont in the best possible light, and its enemies – the Pope, the King of Naples and Mazzini (ironically a son of Piedmont himself, being born in Genoa) – in the worst. Surely it was only right that Italy should have a constitution and civil service, as well as a legal and financial system, based closely on that of gallant Piedmont? Those who disagreed had no choice in the matter, especially since the army was controlled by Piedmont.

Conclusion

In 1861 Piedmont's Prime Minister d'Azeglio had remarked: 'Italy is made, now we must make Italians.' It seems appropriate to end with another less often quoted remark which shows that he at least was aware of the long and difficult task that lay ahead for the government in 1861. It took a long time to achieve unification, and many had hoped that it would come about earlier, during the revolutions of 1848–9 if not before. But d'Azeglio realised that much more time was needed when he said: 'To make an Italy out of Italians, one must not be in a hurry.'

Despite the rhetoric of the *Risorgimento*, Italy was still a country with strong local loyalties and identities. People did not automatically become 'Italians' in 1861 or 1866 or 1870, or even later, just because they lived in Italy. They remained first and foremost Piedmontese, Neapolitans, Tuscans, Lombards or Venetians. To make Italy into a single nation was going to be a slow process. Unification, so long awaited, was no more than a first step.

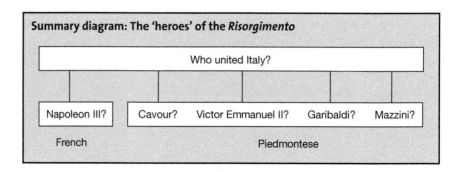

Summary diagram: The 'heroes' of the *Risorgimento*

Chapter summary

Giuseppe Mazzini, the man who had hoped and worked for Italian unity for so long, wrote a devastating critique of the new Italian state in 1871, pointing out that unification had come about not by the united efforts of Italians but by warfare and French intervention. The result was a state controlled by the rich in the interests of the rich. Despite his words, a tradition soon grew up that unification had come about because of a glorious and noble resurgence of the spirit of the Italian people – by the *Risorgimento*. Such myth-making was designed to give members of the new Italian state self-confidence, and also to ensure their support of that state.

The historical reality, however, was that unification had resulted more from the clashes, than the co-operation, of the leading figures involved in unification, especially the politician Cavour and the solider Garibaldi. Yet other figures played important roles too, including the king of Piedmont, Victor Emmanuel II, and the French emperor, Napoleon III. Especial note must also be taken of the role of Piedmont.

Refresher questions

Use these questions to remind yourself of the key material covered in this chapter.

1 How far did the creation of the Kingdom of Italy fulfil the agenda of Mazzini and 'Young Italy'?

2 What is the meaning of *Risorgimento*?

3 What does the term *Risorgimento* imply about the process of unification?

4 Why have so many non-Italian historians criticised the notion of the *Risorgimento*?

5 How much hostility was there between Cavour and Garibaldi?

6 Did Mazzini play an important role in the unification of Italy?

7 How important was Victor Emmanuel II's role in unification?

8 Was the input of Napoleon III crucial to Italian unification?

9 Why was Piedmont the Italian state to spearhead unification?

10 Why did the creation of the Italian nation-state not automatically produce 'Italians'?

 # Question practice

ESSAY QUESTIONS

1 'The new Kingdom of Italy was simply an expanded Piedmont.' How far do you agree?

2 Which of the following was of greater importance in the unification of Italy? i) The impact of Prussia's war in 1866. ii) The impact of Prussia's war in 1870–1. Explain your answer with reference to both i) and ii).

3 How accurate is it to say that it was Piedmont and the Piedmontese that produced Italian unification in the years 1848–70?

4 'The idea behind the *Risorgimento*, that a glorious Italian resurgence produced unification, is largely a myth.' How far do you agree with this statement?

INTERPRETATION QUESTION

1 Read the interpretation and then answer the question that follows. 'The new Italy emerged out of the basic conflict of the opposing patriotic forces and the personal hostility of their leaders, not the complementary and harmonious roles of the four heroic leaders.' (From *A History of Italy 1700–1860*, S. Woolf, 1992.) Evaluate the strengths and limitations of this interpretation, making reference to other interpretations you have studied.

Edexcel A level History

Essay guidance

Edexcel's Paper 2, Option 2D.1: The unification of Italy, *c.*1830–70 is assessed by an exam comprising two sections:

- Section A tests the depth of your historical knowledge through source analysis (see page 144 for guidance on this).
- Section B requires you to write one essay from a choice of two from your own knowledge.

The following advice relates to Paper 2, Section B. It is relevant to A level and AS level questions. Generally, the AS exam is similar to the A level exam. Both examine the same content and require similar skills; nonetheless, there are differences, which are discussed below.

Essay skills

In order to get a high grade in Section B of Paper 2 your essay must contain four essential qualities:

- focused analysis
- relevant detail
- supported judgement
- organisation, coherence and clarity.

This section focuses on the following aspects of exam technique:

- understanding the nature of the question
- planning an answer to the question set
- writing a focused introduction
- deploying relevant detail
- writing analytically
- reaching a supported judgement.

The nature of the question

Section B questions are designed to test the depth of your historical knowledge. Therefore, they can focus on relatively short periods, or single events, or indeed on the whole period from 1830 to 1870. Moreover,

they can focus on different historical processes or 'concepts'. These include:

- cause
- consequence
- change/continuity
- similarity/difference
- significance.

These different question focuses require slightly different approaches:

Cause	1 'The idea that a glorious Italian resurgence produced unification *c.*1830–70 is largely a myth.' How far do you agree with this statement in relation to the *Risorgimento*?
Consequence	2 To what extent was Italian unification the consequence of Garibaldi's actions up to 1861?
Continuity and change	3 How accurate is it to say that very little progress was made in unifying Italians in the period from 1820 to 1848, compared to progress from 1849 to 1861?
Similarities and differences	4 'The actions and attitudes of Garibaldi and Cavour radically differed in the years 1850–61'. How far do you agree with this statement?
Significance	5 'Garibaldi's contribution to the unification of Italy has been exaggerated: he caused more problems than he solved.' How far do you agree with this statement?

Some questions include a 'stated factor'. The most common type of stated factor question would ask how far one factor caused something. For example, the first question in the table asks:

'The idea that a glorious Italian resurgence produced unification *c.*1830–70 is largely a myth.' How far do you agree with this statement in relation to the *Risorgimento*?

In this type of question you would be expected to evaluate the importance of 'the *Risorgimento*' – the 'stated factor' – compared to other factors.

AS and A level questions

AS level questions are generally similar to A level questions. However, the wording of AS questions will be slightly less complex than the wording of A level questions.

A level question	AS level question	Differences
How far do you agree that the weaknesses and divisions of the nationalists were the principal reasons for the failure of the 1848 revolutions in Italy?	How accurate is it to say that very little progress was made in unifying Italians in the period from 1820 to 1848?	The AS question asks how accurate it is to say that there was very little progress made. The A level question asks you to make the more complex judgement: how far were the weaknesses and divisions of the nationalists 'the principal reasons'?

To achieve the highest level at A level, you will have to deal with the full complexity of the question. For example, if you were dealing with question 4, on the extent to which Garibaldi and Cavour's actions and attitudes differed, you would have to deal with the question of how far these were 'radically different', not merely what their attitudes and actions were.

Planning your answer

It is crucial that you understand the focus of the question. Therefore, read the question carefully before you start planning. Check:

- The chronological focus: which years should your essay deal with?
- The topic focus: what aspect of your course does the question deal with?
- The conceptual focus: is this a causes, consequences, change/continuity, similarity/difference or significance question?

Your plan should reflect the task that you have been set. Section B asks you to write an analytical, coherent and well-structured essay from your own knowledge, which reaches a supported conclusion in around 40 minutes:

- To ensure that your essay is coherent and well structured, it should comprise a series of paragraphs, each focusing on a different point.
- Your paragraphs should come in a logical order. For example, you could write your paragraphs in order of importance, so you begin with the most important issues and end with the least important.
- In essays where there is a 'stated factor', it is a good idea to start with the stated factor before moving on to the other points.
- To make sure you keep to time, you should aim to write three or four paragraphs plus an introduction and a conclusion.

The opening paragraph

The opening paragraph should do four main things:

- answer the question directly
- set out your essential argument
- outline the factors or issues that you will discuss
- define key terms used in the question – where necessary.

Different questions require you to define different terms, for example:

A level question	Key term
How far do you agree that the weaknesses and divisions of the nationalists were the principal reasons for the failure of the 1848 revolutions in Italy?	In this example, it is worth defining 'principal reasons'.

Here's an example introduction in answer to question 2 in the table on page 140:

To what extent was Italian unification the consequence of Garibaldi's actions up to 1861?

Garibaldi's actions certainly contributed to Italian unification[1]. Garibaldi's ability to inspire followers, his expedition to Sicily with

'The Thousand' and his military successes contributed towards the development of Italian unification. Yet, the importance of Cavour's actions, particularly his invasion of the Papal States, cannot be underestimated[2]. Clearly, Garibaldi's actions had major effects, although he could not have succeeded without Cavour[3].

1 The essay starts with a clear answer to the question.
2 This sentence simultaneously defines Garibaldi's actions and sets out the key areas the essay will consider.
3 Finally, the essential argument is stated.

The opening paragraph: advice

- Don't write more than a couple of sentences on general background knowledge. This is unlikely to focus explicitly on the question.
- After defining key terms, refer back to these definitions when justifying your conclusion.
- The introduction should reflect the rest of the essay. Don't make one argument in your introduction, then make a different argument in the essay.

Deploying relevant detail

Paper 2 tests the depth of your historical knowledge. Therefore, you will need to deploy historical detail. In the main body of your essay your paragraphs should begin with a clear point, be full of relevant detail and end with explanation or evaluation. A detailed answer might include statistics, proper names, dates and technical terms. For example, if you were writing a paragraph about the war of 1859, you might include statistics dealing with the numbers of soldiers in armies and soldiers who died during the war.

Writing analytically

The quality of your analysis is one of the key factors that determines the mark you achieve. Writing analytically means clearly showing the relationships between the ideas in your essay. Analysis includes two key skills: explanation and evaluation.

Explanation

Explanation means giving reasons. An explanatory sentence has three parts:

- a claim: a statement that something is true or false
- a reason: a statement that justifies the claim
- a relationship: a word or phrase that shows the relationship between the claim and the reason.

Imagine you are answering question 3 in the table on page 140:

> How accurate is it to say that very little progress was made in unifying Italians in the period from 1820 to 1848, compared to progress from 1849 to 1861?

Your paragraph on Cavour's actions should start with a clear point, which would be supported by a series of examples. Finally, you would round off the paragraph with some explanation:

Therefore, Cavour's actions, especially his invasion of the Papal States, contributed to the unification of Italy[1] because[2] these, together with Garibaldi handing over his territories, made the unification of Italy under the kingdom of Victor Emmanuel and his Piedmontese army a reality[3].

1 Claim.   2 Relationship.   3 Reason.

Make sure of the following:

- The reason you give genuinely justifies the claim you have made.
- Your explanation is focused on the question.

Reaching a supported judgement

Finally, your essay should reach a supported judgement. The obvious place to do this is in the conclusion of your essay. Even so, the judgement should reflect the findings of your essay. The conclusion should present:

- a clear judgement that answers the question
- an evaluation of the evidence that supports the judgement.

Finally, the evaluation should reflect valid criteria.

Evaluation and criteria

Evaluation means weighing up to reach a judgement. Therefore, evaluation requires you to:

- summarise both sides of the issue
- reach a conclusion that reflects the proper weight of both sides.

So, for question 2 in the table on page 140:

To what extent was Italian unification the consequence of Garibaldi's actions up to 1861?

the conclusion might look like this:

In conclusion, Garibaldi's actions partially contributed to Italian unification[1]. Clearly, Garibaldi's charisma and relaxed leadership style inspired many followers, including his Red Shirts and many others marching with him, and this led to military successes in Naples and Sicily[2]. However, his followers had a tendency to desert him during times of inaction, and Garibaldi's conquest of the south could also be said to be down to the incompetence, and lack of enthusiasm to retaliate, of the enemy.

Additionally, Cavour's action of sending a Piedmontese army to invade the Papal States forestalled Garibaldi's progress north so he could meet Victor Emmanuel in Neapolitan territory instead[3]. Therefore, by 1861, Garibaldi's actions led to the partial unification of Italy because although he conquered the south, a fully unified Italy would not have been successful had Cavour not acted as well[4].

1. The conclusion starts with a clear judgement that answers the question.
2. This sentence considers the ways in which modernisation was achieved, presenting a summary of the evidence.
3. The conclusion also considers evidence of the limits of modernisation.
4. The essay ends with a final judgement that is supported by the evidence of the essay.

The judgement is supported in part by evaluating the evidence, and in part by linking it to valid criteria. In this case, the criterion is the definition of Garibaldi's actions by 1861 set out in the introduction. Significantly, this criterion is specific to this essay, and different essays will require you to think of different criteria to help you make your judgement.

Sources guidance

Edexcel's Paper 2, Option 2D.1: The unification of Italy, c.1830–70 is assessed by an exam comprising two sections:

- Section A tests the depth of your historical knowledge through source analysis.
- Section B requires you to write one essay from a choice of two from your own knowledge (see page 140 for guidance on this).

The following advice relates to Paper 2, Section A. It is relevant to A level and AS level questions. Generally, the AS exam is similar to the A level exam. Both examine the same content and require similar skills; nonetheless, there are differences, which are discussed below.

The questions in Paper 2, Section A, are structured differently in the A level and AS exams.

AS exam	Full A level exam
Section A: contains one compulsory question divided into two parts. Part a) is worth 8 marks. It focuses on the value of a single source for a specific enquiry. Part b) is worth 12 marks. It asks you to weigh the value of a single source for a specific enquiry. Together the two sources will comprise about 350 words.	Section A: contains a single compulsory question worth 20 marks. The question asks you to evaluate the usefulness of two sources for a specific historical enquiry. Together the two sources will comprise about 400 words.
Questions will start with the following stem: a) Why is Source 1 valuable to the historian for an enquiry about … ? b) How much weight do you give the evidence of Source 2 for an enquiry into … ?	Questions will start with the following stem: **1** How far could the historian make use of Sources 1 and 2 together to investigate … ?

Edexcel style questions

AS style question

Study Sources 1 and 2 before you answer this question.

a) Why is Source 1 valuable to the historian for an enquiry into relations between Cavour and Garibaldi in 1860–1?

Explain your answer using the source, the information given about it and your own knowledge of the historical context.

b) How much weight do you give the evidence of Source 2 for an enquiry into popular attitudes towards Garibaldi in 1849?

Explain your answer using the source, the information given about it and your own knowledge of the historical context.

A level style question

Study Sources 1 and 2 before you answer this question.

How far could the historian make use of Sources 1 and 2 together to investigate the role of Garibaldi in fostering the unification of Italy by 1861?

Explain your answer using both sources, the information given about them and your own knowledge of the historical context.

Sources 1 and 2

SOURCE 1

Cavour writing to Constantino Nigra, the Piedmontese minister in Paris, 12 July 1860. Quoted in Denis Mack Smith, *The Making of Italy*, Palgrave Macmillan, 1988, pp. 325–6.

Garibaldi has become intoxicated by success and by the praise showered on him all over Europe. He is planning the wildest, not to say absurdest schemes. As he remains devoted to King Victor Emmanuel, he will not help Mazzini or republicanism. But he feels it his vocation to liberate all Italy, stage by stage, before turning her over to the King. He is thus putting off the day when Sicily will demand annexation to Piedmont,

for he wants to keep the dictatorial powers which will enable him to raise an army to conquer first Naples, then Rome, and in the end Venice. Some people even maintain that in private conversation he does not conceal his intention of taking Nice back from France! … The government here has no influence on him. On the contrary he mistrusts everybody whom he imagines to be in touch with us …

SOURCE 2

From a description of Garibaldi by a Dutch artist in 1849, quoted in George Macaulay Trevelyan, *Garibaldi's Defence of the Roman Republic*, Cosimo, 2008, p. 117.

Garibaldi entered through the gate. It was the first time I had seen the man whose name everyone in Rome knew and in whom many had placed their hopes. Of middle height, well built, broad shouldered, his square chest gives a sense of power – he stood there before us; his blue eyes, verging on violet, surveyed in one glance the entire group. Those eyes had something remarkable … they contrasted curiously with those dark sparkling eyes of his Italian soldiers, and his light chestnut brown

hair, which fell loosely over his shoulders, contrasting with their shining black curls. His face was burnt red with the sun and his face covered with freckles.

A heavy moustache and a light blonde beard ending in two points gave a military expression to his face. Most striking was his broad nose which has caused him to be given the name of Leone and indeed made one think of a lion …

Understanding the questions

- To answer the question successfully you must understand how the question works.
- The question is written precisely in order to make sure that you understand the task. Each part of the question has a specific meaning.
- You must use the source, the information given about the source and your own knowledge of the historical context when answering the question.

Understanding the AS question

a) Why is Source 1 valuable to the historian for an enquiry[1] into relations between Cavour and Garibaldi in 1860–1[2]?

Explain your answer using the source, the information given about it and your own knowledge of the historical context.

1   You must focus on the reasons why the source could be helpful to a historian. Indeed, you can get maximum marks without considering the source's limitations.
2   The final part of the question focuses on a specific topic that a historian might investigate. In this case: 'relations between Cavour and Garibaldi in 1860–1'.

b) How much weight do you give the evidence of Source 2[1] for an enquiry[2] into popular attitudes towards Garibaldi in 1849[3]?

Explain your answer using the source, the information given about it and your own knowledge of the historical context.

1   This question focuses on evaluating the extent to which the source contains evidence. Therefore, you must consider the ways in which the source is valuable and the limitations of the source.
2   This is the essence of the task: you must focus on what a historian could legitimately conclude from studying this source.
3   This is the specific topic that you are considering the source for: 'popular attitudes towards Garibaldi in 1849'.

Understanding the A level question

How far[1] could the historian make use of Sources 1 and 2[2] together[3] to investigate the role of Garibaldi in fostering the unification of Italy by 1861[4]?

Explain your answer using both sources, the information given about them and your own knowledge of the historical context[5].

1   You must evaluate the extent of something, rather than giving a simple 'yes' or 'no' answer.
2   This is the essence of the task: you must focus on what a historian could legitimately conclude from studying these sources.
3   You must examine the sources as a pair and make a judgement about both sources, rather than simply making separate judgements about each source.

4   The final part of the question focuses on a specific topic that a historian might investigate. In this case: 'the unification of Italy by 1861'.
5   This instruction lists the resources you should use: the sources, the information given about the sources and your own knowledge of the historical context that you have learnt during the course.

Source skills

Generally, Section A of Paper 2 tests your ability to evaluate source material. More specifically, the sources presented in Section A will be taken from the period that you have studied: 1830–70, or be written by people who witnessed these events. Your job is to analyse the sources by reading them in the context of the values and assumptions of the society and the period that produced them.

Examiners will mark your work by focusing on the extent to which you are able to:

• Interpret and analyse source material:
   – At a basic level, this means that you can understand the sources and select, copy, paraphrase and summarise the source or sources to help answer the question.
   – At a higher level, your interpretation of the sources includes the ability to explain, analyse and make inferences based on the sources.
   – At the highest levels, you will be expected to analyse the source in a sophisticated way. This includes the ability to distinguish between information, opinions and arguments contained in the sources.
• Deploy knowledge of historical context in relation to the sources:
   – At a basic level, this means the ability to link the sources to your knowledge of the context in which the source was written, using this knowledge to expand or support the information contained in the sources.
   – At a higher level, you will be able to use your contextual knowledge to make inferences, and to expand, support or challenge the details mentioned in the sources.

– At the highest levels, you will be able to examine the value and limits of the material contained in the sources by interpreting the sources in the context of the values and assumptions of the society that produced them.
- Evaluate the usefulness and weight of the source material:
  – At a basic level, evaluation of the source will be based on simplistic criteria about reliability and bias.
  – At a higher level, evaluation of the source will be based on the nature and purpose of the source.
  – At the highest levels, evaluation of the source will be based on a valid criterion that is justified in the course of the essay. You will also be able to distinguish between the value of different aspects of the sources.

Make sure your source evaluation is sophisticated. Avoid crude statements about bias, and avoid simplistic assumptions such as that a source written immediately after an event is reliable, whereas a source written years later is unreliable.

Try to see things through the eyes of the writer:

- How does the writer understand the world?
- What assumptions does the writer have?
- Who is the writer trying to influence?
- What views is the writer trying to challenge?

Basic skill: comprehension

The most basic source skill is comprehension: understanding what the sources mean. There are a variety of techniques that you can use to aid comprehension. For example, you could read the sources included in this book and in past papers:

- Read the sources out loud.
- Look up any words that you don't understand and make a glossary.
- Make flash cards containing brief biographies of the writers of the sources.

You can demonstrate comprehension by copying, paraphrasing and summarising the sources. However, keep this to the minimum as comprehension is a low-level skill and you need to leave room for higher-level skills.

Advanced skill: contextualising the sources

First, to analyse the sources correctly you need to understand them in the context in which they were written. People in Italy in the 1800s saw the world differently from people in early twenty-first-century Britain. The sources reflect this. Your job is to understand the values and assumptions behind the source.

- One way of contextualising the sources is to consider the nature, origins and purpose of the sources. However, this can lead to formulaic responses.
- An alternative is to consider two levels of context. First, you should establish the general context. In this case, Sources 1 and 2 refer to a period in which Garibaldi and Cavour were emerging as key figures driving the unification of Italy. Second, you can look for specific references to contemporary events or debates in the sources. For example:

Sources 1 and 2 both refer to Garibaldi. They reflect criticisms of Garibaldi's actions (Source 1), but also his devotion to seeing Italy unified, and indeed the Italian people's devotion to him (Source 2). Another important contextual reference in Source 1 is the reference to Victor Emmanuel, Mazzini and republicanism: Garibaldi had been a republican and had only lately become a royalist. Cavour was not entirely sure whether this change of heart was genuine.

Use context to make judgements

- Start by establishing the general context of the source:
  - Ask yourself: what was going on at the time when the source was written, or the time of the events described in the source?
  - What are the key debates that the source might be contributing to?
- Next, look for key words and phrases that establish the specific context. Does the source refer to specific people, events or books that might be important?
- Make sure your contextualisation focuses on the question.
- Use the context when evaluating the usefulness and limitations of the source.

For example:

How far could the historian make use of Sources 1 and 2 together to investigate the role of Garibaldi in fostering the unification of Italy by 1861?

Source 1 is valuable to a historian investigating the role of Garibaldi in the unification of Italy because it shows how concerned Cavour was about Garibaldi's military actions and his overwhelming desire to 'liberate all Italy, stage by stage'. Moreover, Source 2 is valuable because it shows how recognisable Garibaldi was as a powerful figure. Although Source 2 was written by a Dutch artist, and not an Italian, the artist notes that this was a man 'whose name everyone in Rome knew and in whom many had placed their hopes'. This indicates that Garibaldi's actions had a far-reaching impact.

OCR A level History

Essay guidance

The assessment of OCR Units Y215 and Y245: Italy and Unification 1789–1896 depends on whether you are studying it for AS or A level:

- for the AS exam, you will answer one essay question from a choice of two, and one interpretation question, for which there is no choice
- for the A level exam, you will answer one essay question from a choice of two, and one shorter essay question, also from a choice of two.

The guidance below is for answering both AS and A level essay questions. Guidance for the shorter essay question is at the end of this section. Guidance on answering interpretation questions is on page 154.

For both OCR AS and A level History, the types of essay questions set and the skills required to achieve a high grade for Unit Group 2 are the same. The skills are made very clear by both mark schemes, which emphasise that the answer must:

- focus on the demands of the question
- be supported by accurate and relevant factual knowledge
- be analytical and logical
- reach a supported judgement about the issue in the question.

There are a number of skills that you will need to develop to reach the higher levels in the marking bands:

- understand the wording of the question
- plan an answer to the question set
- write a focused opening paragraph
- avoid irrelevance and description
- write analytically
- write a conclusion which reaches a supported judgement based on the argument in the main body of the essay.

These skills will be developed in the section below, but are further developed in the 'Period Study' chapters of the *OCR A level History* series (British Period Studies and Enquiries).

Understanding the wording of the question

To stay focused on the question set, it is important to read the question carefully and focus on the key words and phrases. Unless you directly address the demands of the question you will not score highly. Remember, in questions where there is a named factor you must write a good analytical paragraph about the given factor, even if you argue that it was not the most important.

Types of AS and A level questions you might find in the exams	The factors and issues you would need to consider in answering them
1 Assess the reasons why the revolutions of 1848–9 in Italy ended in failure.	Weigh up the relative importance of a range of factors as to why the 1848–9 revolutions failed.
2 To what extent was the role of foreign powers the most important reason for the unification of Italy by 1871?	Weigh up the relative importance of a range of factors, including comparing the importance of foreign powers with other factors.
3 'The leadership of Cavour was the most important reason for the unification of Italy by 1871.' How far do you agree?	Weigh up the relative importance of a range of factors, including comparing the importance of Cavour's leadership with other issues to reach a balanced judgement.
4 How successful was Garibaldi as a revolutionary leader?	This question requires you to make a judgement about Garibaldi as a revolutionary leader. Instead of thinking about factors, you would

need to think about issues such as:

- Garibaldi's success in taking Sicily and Naples and the consequences of his actions
- His decision to surrender Sicily and Naples to Victor Emmanuel and the avoidance of civil war
- His devotion to the idea of unity
- Garibaldi's role as a war leader and the organisation of the war in Sicily and Naples
- His handling of particular issues and crises
- His charisma, enthusiasm and inspiration.

Planning an answer

Many plans simply list dates and events – this should be avoided as it encourages a descriptive or narrative answer, rather than an analytical answer. The plan should be an outline of your argument; this means you need to think carefully about the issues you intend to discuss and their relative importance before you start writing your answer. It should therefore be a list of the factors or issues you are going to discuss and a comment on their relative importance.

For question 1 in the table, your plan might look something like this:

- Lack of co-operation between the revolutionary groups.
- Belief that nationalism could develop only after constitutional governments had been established.
- Lack of national leader.
- Confusion of ideologies: moderate, extremist, republican, liberal, monarchist.
- Provisional governments were inexperienced and lacked resources.
- Lack of popular support among the masses.
- Military superiority of Austria; superior in numbers and better equipped; only when they were driven out was unity possible.

The opening paragraph

Many students spend time 'setting the scene'; the opening paragraph becomes little more than an introduction to the topic – this should be avoided. Instead, make it clear what your argument is going to be. Offer your view about the issue in the question – what was the most important reason for the failure of the 1848–9 revolutions – and then introduce the other issues you intend to discuss. In the plan it is suggested that Austrian military superiority was the most important factor. This should be made clear in the opening paragraph, with a brief comment as to why – perhaps that the resources, leadership and numerical superiority meant that in any conflict they were bound to win; it was with Austrian intervention and support that the old regimes were restored. This will give the examiner a clear overview of your essay, rather than it being a 'mystery tour' where the argument becomes clear only at the end. You should also refer to any important issues that the question raises. For example:

There are a number of reasons why the 1848–9 revolutions failed, including a lack of co-operation between the revolutions and the lack of popular support for revolution[1]. However, the most important reason was the military strength of Austria, which was superior in resources, numbers and leadership[2]. This was particularly important as it was Austrian forces that drove out the revolutionary groups and restored the old regimes[3].

1 The student is aware that there were a number of important reasons.
2 The student offers a clear view as to what they consider to be the most important reason – a thesis is offered.
3 There is a brief justification to support the thesis.

Avoid irrelevance and description

A well-prepared plan will stop you from simply writing all you know about why the revolutions failed and force you to weigh up the role of a range of factors. Similarly, it should also help prevent you from simply writing about the events of the 1848–9 revolutions. You will not lose marks if you do that, but neither will you gain any credit, and you will waste valuable time.

Write analytically

This is perhaps the hardest, but most important skill you need to develop. An analytical approach can be helped by ensuring that the opening sentence of each paragraph introduces an idea, which directly answers the question and is not just a piece of factual information. In a very strong answer it should be possible to simply read the opening sentences of all the paragraphs and know what argument is being put forward.

If we look at question 2, on the role of foreign powers in bringing about unification (see page 149), the following are possible sentences with which to start paragraphs:

- The role of France was crucial in driving Austria out of parts of Italy, both in 1859 and in 1866 …
- Without the Austro-Prussian War of 1866, the Austrian presence in Venetia would not have been removed …
- Italy was unified because Victor Emmanuel became a popular, liberal leader and worked with Cavour …
- It was only through Cavour's diplomacy and master plan that Sardinia obtained the allies needed for unification …

You would then go on to discuss both sides of the argument raised by the opening sentence, using relevant knowledge about the issue to support each side of the argument. The final sentences of the paragraph would reach a judgement on the role played by the factor you are discussing in the unification of Italy. This approach would ensure that the final sentence of each paragraph links back to the actual question you are answering. If you can do this for each paragraph you will have a series of mini-essays, which discuss a factor and reach a conclusion or judgement about the importance of that factor or issue. For example:

Lacking sufficient military strength on its own, French support for Piedmont was crucial in 1859 in securing Lombardy[1]. The sending of 120,000 men to Lombardy was vitally important in overrunning the province and defeating the Austrians at Magenta and Solferino. However, there were limits to the French contribution as they were unable to fulfil their agreement to remove the Austrians from Venetia because the Austrians withdrew to their strongly fortified positions and Napoleon made peace, fearing that a long war would be used by Prussia to attack France[2].

1 The sentence puts forward a clear view that French support was crucial as Piedmont lacked the necessary military strength to defeat Austria.
2 The claim that it was successful in driving Austria out of only parts of Italy in 1859 is developed.

The conclusion

The conclusion provides the opportunity to bring together all the interim judgements to reach an overall judgement about the question. Using the interim judgements will ensure that your conclusion is based on the argument in the main body of the essay and does not offer a different view. For the essay answering question 1 (see page 149), you can decide what was the most important factor in the failure of the 1848–9 revolutions, but for questions 2 and 3 you will need to comment on the importance of the named factor – the role of foreign powers and the leadership of Cavour – as well as explain why you think a different factor is more important, if that has been your line of argument. Or, if you think the named factor is the most important, you would need to explain why that was more important than the other factors or issues you have discussed.

Consider the following conclusion to question 2: To what extent was the role of foreign powers the most important reason for the unification of Italy by 1871?

Although the intervention of foreign powers, most notably France and Prussia, was important in securing much of northern Italy, it was not the most important factor in unification[1].

Foreign powers did not secure the south for Italy: that was the work of Garibaldi, but without popular support for unity his success may not have occurred. Moreover, the work of other individuals, most notably Cavour and Victor Emmanuel II, was important, as Cavour modernised Piedmont so that it could provide the leadership, while Victor Emmanuel provided the crucial figurehead for the movement for unity. Therefore, although foreign aid was important militarily, it would not have brought about unification on its own; that required leadership and support from within Italy[2].

1 This is a strong conclusion because it considers the importance of the named factor – the role of foreign powers – but weighs that up against a range of other factors to reach an overall judgement.
2 It is also able to show links between the other factors to reach a balanced judgement, which brings in a range of issues, showing the interplay between them.

How to write a good essay for the A level short answer questions

This question will require you to weigh up the importance of two factors or issues in relation to an event or a development. For example:

Which had the greater consequences for the development of nationalism in Italy?

(i) Napoleon's actions in Italy.

(ii) The Vienna Settlement of 1815.

Explain your answer with reference to both (i) and (ii).

As with the long essays, the skills required are made very clear by the mark scheme, which emphasises that the answer must:

- analyse the two issues
- evaluate the two issues
- support your analysis and evaluation with detailed and accurate knowledge
- reach a supported judgement as to which factor was more important in relation to the issue in the question.

The skills required are very similar to those for the longer essays. However, there is no need for an introduction, nor are you required to compare the two factors or issues in the main body of the essay, although either approach can still score full marks. For example, an opening paragraph could be:

Napoleon's actions in Italy had a significant consequence in the development of nationalism in Italy as they resulted in the belief that Italy could become a unitary state[1]. The rearrangement of state boundaries ended up with the peninsula being divided into only three parts, with Piedmont annexed to France, and the establishment of the kingdom of Italy and the kingdom of Naples, which gave Italy some sort of unity, even if it was through conquest[2]. Its impact was also far reaching as laws were standardised and representative government was introduced, which gave the middle class a chance to discuss politics and become involved in political affairs on a national basis[3].

1 The answer explains one of the consequences of Napoleon's actions.
2 The implications of this development are considered.
3 The wider implications are hinted at. This could be developed and the actions of the King of Naples in 1815 used to show the progress that had been made, as he was able to call on the people of the peninsula to support him in making Italy united and independent.

The answer could go on and argue how Napoleon's actions reduced the power of the Church and Pope, how a new middle class began to be created, which would be crucial in the development of nationalism, and how the peasants were freed from many of their feudal ties.

Most importantly, the conclusion must reach a supported judgement as to the relative importance of the factors in relation to the issue in the question. For example:

Both of the issues had a significant impact on the development of nationalism. The Vienna Settlement had a more negative impact on the development of nationalism as it resulted in the reassembling of Italy as it had been in pre-Napoleonic times, whereas Napoleon's actions, despite conquest, had a positive impact in both the short and long term, and therefore had the greater impact[1]. Although the unity that had been created under Napoleon had been artificial, the possibility of a united Italy was seen, whereas the Vienna Settlement undid those developments. It reinstated most of the ruling families, who soon re-established absolutist rule and suppressed nationalist developments, all of which was contrary to the ideas and developments that had grown during the Napoleonic period[2].

1 The response explains the relative importance of the two factors and offers a clear view.
2 The response supports the view offered in the opening sentence and therefore reaches a supported judgement.

Interpretations guidance

How to write a good essay

The guidance below is for answering the AS interpretation questions on Unit Y245: Italy and Unification 1789–1896. Guidance on answering essay questions is on page 149.

The OCR specification outlines the two key topics from which the interpretation question will be drawn. For this book these are:

- The revolutions of 1848–9 and their aftermath.
- The *Risorgimento* and the establishment of a new kingdom of Italy 1850–61.

The specification also lists the main debates to consider.

It is also worth remembering that this is an AS unit and not an A level historiography paper. The aim of this element of the unit is to develop an awareness that the past can be interpreted in different ways.

The question will require you to assess the strengths and limitations of ahistorian's interpretation of an issue related to one of the specified key topics.

You should be able to place the interpretation within the context of the wider historical debate on the key topic. However, you will *not* be required to know the names of individual historians associated with the debate or to have studied the specific books of any historians. It may even be counter-productive to be aware of particular historians' views, as this may lead you to simply describe their view, rather than analyse the given interpretation.

There are a number of skills you need to develop if you are to reach the higher levels in the mark bands:

- To be able to understand the wording of the question.
- To be able to explain the interpretation and how it fits into the debate about the issue or topic.
- To be able to consider both the strengths and weaknesses of the interpretation by using your own knowledge of the topic.

Here is an example of a question you will face in the exam:

> Read the interpretation and then answer the question that follows:
>
> 'More convincing is the view he [Cavour] united Italy not so much as the result of intention or conviction but more through force of circumstances.'
>
> (From A. Stiles, *The Unification of Italy 1815–1870*, 2006.)
>
> Evaluate the strengths and limitations of this interpretation, making reference to other interpretations that you have studied.

Approaching the question

There are several steps to take to answer this question:

1 Explain the interpretation and put it into the context of the debate on the topic

In the first paragraph, you should explain the interpretation and the view it is putting forward. This paragraph places the interpretation in the context of the historical debate and explains any key words or phrases relating to the given interpretation. A suggested opening might be as follows:

The interpretation puts forward the view that there is more than one possible view for Cavour's decision to unite Italy in 1861[1]. This interpretation argues that Cavour had no clear plan, or even desire, to unite Italy but was forced into it by circumstances or events that put him under pressure or gave him little choice but to intervene[2]. The interpretation suggests that this was more important than the view of nineteenth-century historians who believed that great men could change history and therefore who saw Cavour as the patriot who made Italy[3].

1 The opening two sentences are clearly focused on the given interpretation. They clearly explain that there is more than one interpretation for the unification of Italy in 1861, but there is no detailed own knowledge added at this point.
2 The second sentence explains what is meant by 'force of circumstances'.

3 The last sentence begins to place the concept of circumstances in the wider historical debate and suggests that this historian's emphasis on it challenges the view that intention and conviction were less important factors.

In order to place Stiles' view in the context of the debate about the importance of various issues, you could go on to suggest that some have argued that Cavour had a clear and consistent aim of uniting Italy under the Sardinian monarchy, or that he had a master plan to bring about unification.

2 Consider the strengths of the interpretation

In the second paragraph, consider the strengths of the interpretation by bringing in your own knowledge that supports the given view. A suggested response might start as follows when considering the strengths of the view:

There is considerable merit to Stiles' view as although it acknowledges that historians are divided in their interpretation about why Cavour united Italy in 1861, it offers a clear view that it was due to circumstances[1]. The interpretation is correct as Cavour sent troops to the Crimea only because he was pressurised by Britain and France, and because he heard there were plans to replace him as prime minister, not because he had a master plan to gain the French and British as allies. Moreover, in 1860–1 Cavour was fortunate that Garibaldi, after his invasion of Sicily and Naples, continued to advance towards the Papal States, which would have brought in Austria and France, which forced him to intervene and led to the uniting of Italy[2]. These examples show how it was circumstances rather than a clear plan that brought Cavour to intervene and ultimately bring about a united Italy[3].

1 The answer clearly focuses on the strength of the given interpretation.
2 The response provides some support for the view in the interpretation from the candidate's own knowledge. This is quite detailed and precise, but could still be developed further in the remainder of the paragraph.

3 The final sentence brings the material together to support the interpretation.

In the remainder of the paragraph you could show how Cavour was driven by circumstances and how this influenced Cavour's decision to annex Sicily once Garibaldi's invasion had been a success, having previously opposed Garibaldi's scheme and having been simply concerned with a north Italian kingdom, fearing that France would not allow Piedmont to expand beyond that.

3 Consider the weaknesses of the interpretation

In the third paragraph, consider the weaknesses of the given interpretation by bringing in knowledge that can challenge the given interpretation and explain what is missing from the interpretation.

A suggested response might start as follows when considering the weaknesses of the view:

However, there are a number of limitations in Stiles' interpretation[1]. Most importantly, it fails to consider the view that Cavour intended to unite Italy under the House of Savoy and created a plan so that Britain and France would act as Piedmont's allies to help bring this about[2]. The interpretation also fails to consider how the master plan gave Sardinia allies that allowed the unification to take place by Cavour's sending troops to the Crimea and then being allowed to explain the case for unification at the Congress of Paris, which ultimately led to the Pact of Plombières[3].

1 The opening makes it very clear that this paragraph will deal with the weaknesses of the interpretation.
2 It explains clearly the first weakness and provides evidence to support the claim. The evidence is not detailed and could be developed, but the answer focuses on explaining the weakness, rather than providing lots of detail.
3 Although more detail could have been provided about the master plan, the answer goes on to explain how allies were gained, and this could be developed in the remainder of the paragraph.

The answer might go on to argue that the securing of allies was important and that Cavour was aware of that. It might also consider that Cavour used Britain to persuade France to allow Italy to expand beyond the agreement reached at Plombières and add the central and southern states, therefore concluding that through diplomacy Cavour was able to transform an unpromising situation in 1859 into a success. The paragraph might therefore suggest that the interpretation provides a partial answer which needs further development.

There is no requirement for you to reach a judgement as to which view you find more convincing or valid.

Assessing the interpretation

In assessing the interpretation you should consider the following:

- Identify and explain the issue being discussed in the interpretation: the role played by Cavour in the unification of Italy.
- Explain the view being put forward in the interpretation: the interpretation is arguing that Cavour did not have a master plan for the unification of Italy and was in fact more concerned with consolidating Piedmontese power in the north than uniting the peninsula, and that unity occurred only because of circumstances.
- Explain how the interpretation fits into the wider debate about the issue: the relative importance of circumstances determining the outcome and nature of the unification, rather than the actions of patriots and great men, such as Cavour and Garibaldi.

In other interpretations you might need to:

- Consider whether there is any particular emphasis within the interpretation that needs explaining or commenting on, for example, if the interpretation says something is 'the only reason' or 'the single most important reason'.
- Comment on any concepts that the interpretation raises, such as 'total war', 'authoritarian system', 'liberalisation'.
- Consider the focus of the interpretation: for example, if an interpretation focuses on an urban viewpoint, what was the rural viewpoint? Is the viewpoint given in the interpretation the same for all areas of society?

Summary: this is what is important for answering interpretation questions:

- Explaining the interpretation.
- Placing it in the context of the wider historical debate about the issue it considers.
- Explaining the strengths *and* weaknesses of the view in the extract.

Glossary of terms

Absolute monarchy   A political system under which a monarch rules without a constitution that limits his powers and without a parliament whose agreement is needed for the making of laws.

Allocution   An official speech giving a warning or advice.

Ambivalence   Contradictory ideas or feelings.

Annexation   The act of taking possession of land and adding it to one's own territory.

Anticlerical   Unsympathetic or hostile to the Church and its clergy.

Armistice   A truce, or ceasefire.

Bedouin   An Arabic word meaning 'desert-dwellers' used to refer to a group of nomadic Arab tribes.

Breech-loading rifles   Rifles whose bullets are loaded through the chamber (or breech) rather than through the barrel (or muzzle). They could be fired four or five times more quickly than muzzle-loaders, and soldiers could load them lying down.

Carbonari   From 'charcoal burners' in Italian, and it has been suggested that the earliest members were men who sold charcoal for domestic fuel. Soon, however, middle-class members predominated.

Ceded   Officially handed over.

Civil marriage   Marriage without a church service.

Clericalist   Supporting the Catholic Church, its clergy and its policies.

Code Napoléon   A set of civil laws, formulated in 1804, which gave France a single legal system and attempted to promote the principle of equal rights for all citizens. (Women, it should be noted, were classified as minors, not as citizens.)

Common land   Land held 'in common' by the people, without individual owners.

Confederation   A loose alliance of states.

Congress   A meeting of several countries to settle key issues.

Conscripted   Forcibly enlisted into the army.

Constituente   A meeting in Rome of representatives from all over Italy.

Constitutional monarchy   A system under which a king is bound by certain agreed restrictions on his power set out in a written document (the constitution).

Contingent   Subject to chance and to the effects of the unforeseen.

Counter-revolutionary   Bringing about a revolution that is opposed to or reverses a former revolution.

Coup   A sudden and violent seizure of power.

Crimean War   A war fought in 1854–6 by Britain and France, with some support from Piedmont, against Russia. Austria decided to remain neutral.

Customs union   An economic agreement whereby two or more states agree to lower or eliminate taxes on the goods they trade with each other.

Dialect   The form of a language found in a particular region.

Dictator   Originally a term used in Ancient Rome to denote a chief magistrate with absolute power, appointed in an emergency.

Dowry   Property or money presented by a bride or her family to her husband.

Dynasty   A succession of powerful rulers from the same family.

Elite   The most important and influential groups in a society, usually those who are wealthy and well educated.

Excommunicated   Excluded from the services and sacraments of the Catholic Church. Those who died excommunicated could not be buried by a priest or in consecrated ground, and so, it was commonly believed, would go to hell.

Expeditionary force   A small army dispatched for a particular mission.

Federal Possessing states that are self-governing in their internal affairs.

Foundling An infant abandoned by its mother and cared for by others.

Freemasonry A secret fraternity providing fellowship and mutual assistance.

French Revolution In the 'great revolution', beginning in 1789, the existing order was overthrown and a republic set up, Louis XVI being executed in 1793.

Garibaldini The soldiers of Garibaldi, also known as legionaries and Red Shirts.

Garrison A body of troops stationed to defend a town or locality.

Genoa The Vienna Settlement of 1815 gave Piedmont control of the former republic of Genoa. This was of great commercial benefit to Piedmont, as Genoa was an important port. But the Genoese were far from impressed, resenting the loss of their former political and commercial independence.

Ghettos Special quarters in Italian towns where Jewish communities were forced to live.

Gross domestic product (GDP) per capita The total production, in terms of goods and services, that each person in a society is responsible for.

Guerrilla fighters Small independent groups, using unorthodox tactics, fighting against regular troops.

Hair shirt A garment made of haircloth, causing discomfort to the body and thereby, according to believers, bringing its wearer closer to God.

Imperialistic Motivated by the desire to dominate or capture other people's territory.

Indirect taxation Tax levied not on income but on goods or services that are bought with income.

Inquisition A much-feared tribunal for prosecuting and punishing heresy, founded in the thirteenth century.

Jesuits Members of the Society of Jesus, a religious order founded in the sixteenth century, who were feared for their complete loyalty to the Papacy.

Knave A scoundrel.

Land reclamation The process of creating new, cultivable land, often by draining it of water.

Latifundia Large estates (from the Latin *latus* meaning wide, and *fundus* meaning estate).

Lay population People who are not members of the clergy.

Legal codes Collections of laws.

Legion The name taken by Garibaldi's irregular troops. Originally it was a division of 3000–6000 men in the army of Ancient Rome. Individual members were called legionaries.

Liberals Members of the elite who wanted progressive change: often constitutional government, the guarantee of individual freedoms and free trade.

Mafia An organised criminal gang, originating as a secret society in thirteenth-century Sicily. In the nineteenth century it took this name (meaning 'swank') and virtually ruled parts of the island, sometimes protecting ordinary peasants from the oppression of corrupt police forces and judges.

Merchant navy A country's commercial shipping fleet.

Milieu A French term, meaning the total social environment.

Minister of the interior The European equivalent of the British home secretary, the minister responsible for, among other things, police and internal security.

Mobilised Organised for a possible war.

Mutual-aid societies Organisations formed by workers who pooled their resources to provide some financial benefits in times of hardship.

Mythologised Exaggerated and idealised, so that it loses touch with reality.

National Society A body set up in 1856 by moderate republicans, aiming to bridge the gap between Mazzini and Garibaldi. Led by the Venetian Daniele Manin, it began to look to the Piedmontese monarchy to spearhead unification.

Neapolitans People from Naples.

Outworkers Those provided with work by a factory but doing it at home.

Palmeritans Natives of Palermo.

Pellagra   A disease causing skin complaints, diarrhoea, self-mutilation and madness that often ends in suicide.

Philosophers   Those who study the nature of reality by using logic and abstract theories.

Piedmontisation   The forcing of the rest of Italy to adopt the laws and customs of Piedmont.

Poncho   A circular cape-like garment with no sleeves or fastenings, and merely a hole for the head.

Precondition   Something without which an event could not have taken place: a 'necessary' factor but not one that is 'sufficient' on its own to explain an event.

Prefects   Appointees, mostly from Piedmont, who had widespread administrative powers – over law and order, local councils, press censorship and the conduct of elections – in the 60 provinces into which Italy was divided.

Progressive   Forward-looking, favouring reform.

Quadrilateral   A group of four heavily defended fortresses near the Austrian border (in Mantua, Peschiera, Verona and Legnago).

Radicals   Reformers who wanted greater change than the liberals, including the overthrow of monarchies.

Reactionary   Favouring a return to previous political conditions and being opposed to political progress.

Red Cross   An international agency founded in 1864 to assist those who were wounded or captured in wars.

Republican democracy   A system under which an elected government controls the affairs of a state, and in which there is no monarch, even as a figurehead.

Restored Monarchs   The rulers whom the Congress of Vienna allowed to return to Italy.

Revisionist historians   Those who disagree with generally accepted historical interpretations and seek to overturn them by arguing differently.

Rhetoric   Fine-sounding, but often exaggerated, language designed to affect the emotions.

Risorgimento   The word first came into use at the end of the eighteenth century and means 'resurgence' or 'rebirth'. Those who first used it suggested that Italian unification would be a noble and heroic affair, paralleling glorious episodes in Italian history such as the Roman Empire and the Renaissance.

Satellites   Weak states dependent on or controlled by a more powerful country.

Second front   An alternative scene of battle, generally diverting the enemy's attention away from the major focus of a war.

Secularist   One who favours the state over the Church.

Spiritual authority   The religious power of the Pope, as head of the Catholic Church.

Synonym   A word that means the same as another word or phrase.

Temporal power   The worldly authority of the Pope, as ruler of the Papal States.

Trade guilds   Associations of craftsmen; early forms of trade unions.

Treadle   A foot-operated lever that applies power to a machine.

Trenchant   Expressed in strong and vigorous language.

Triple Alliance   Under its terms, Germany and Italy would receive the other's support if attacked by France. If Austria-Hungary were at war with Russia, Italy would be neutral, thus giving Austria security on its southern border.

Triumvirate   A governing group of three men.

Viceroy   A ruler exercising authority on behalf of a king or queen.

Vulpine   Like a fox – cunning or sly.

Xenophobia   Hatred of foreigners.

Further reading

General texts

M. Clark, *The Italian Risorgimento* (Routledge, 2009)
A volume in the Seminar Studies series. There is a superb bibliography and a useful collection of source material

Christopher Duggan, *The Force of Destiny: A History of Italy since 1796* (Allen Lane, 2007)
A wide-ranging and interesting account that includes some fascinating quotations from contemporary sources. Chapters 4–16 are particularly relevant

J.A.S. Grenville, *Europe Reshaped 1848–1878*, second edition (Fontana, 2000)
This is solid, reliable and readable. It places Italian unification into its contemporary context, and also has a good section on the relations between Cavour and Garibaldi

H. Hearder, *Italy in the Age of the Risorgimento 1790–1870* (Longman, 1983)
This not only deals clearly with political events but provides useful and interesting background reading on literature and the arts, religious issues and economic and social conditions. There is also a section on sources

Denis Mack Smith, *Modern Italy: A Political History* (Yale University Press, 1997)
A superbly readable introduction that places the period of unification into a wider historical context

Denis Mack Smith, editor, *The Making of Italy* (Palgrave Macmillan, 1988)
An expertly edited collection of key documents

Lucy Riall, *Risorgimento: The History of Italy from Napoleon to Nation State* (Palgrave Macmillan, 2009)
A very useful volume, strong on analysis though not always an easy read. It is best consulted after the events have been studied

Chapter 1

D. Beales and E. Biagini, *The Risorgimento and the Unification of Italy* (Longman, 2002)
This provides an illuminating treatment of the whole period, and especially of 1789–1815

David Gentilcore, 'Peasants and Pellagra in 19th-century Italy', *History Today*, September 2014
Examines the widespread impact of a disease that affected southern Italy for most of the nineteenth century

Chapter 2

Denis Mack Smith, *Mazzini* (Yale University Press, 1996)
A highly detailed but readable biography of one of the leading protagonists

Robert Pearce, 'Mazzini', *History Review*, March 2007, and 'The 1848 Revolutions in Italy', *New Perspective*, vol. 15, no. 2
Specifically written for A level students. *History Review* can be assessed at www.historytoday.com and *New Perspective* at www.history-ontheweb.co.uk

Chapter 3

Harry Hearder, *Cavour* (Routledge, 1994)
An excellent biographical study of the key player in this chapter

Denis Mack Smith, *Cavour* (Littlehampton Book Services, 1985)
A readable and accessible biography

Robert Pearce, 'France and the Unification of Italy', *New Perspective*, vol. 11, no. 3
A brief assessment of Napoleon III's contribution to the unification of Italy

Roger Price, *Napoleon III and the Second Empire* (Routledge, 1997)
A good account of Napoleon III's impact on France and his participation in Italian unification

Mark Rathbone, 'Piedmont in the 1850s', *History Review*, December 2008
An excellent short article, focusing on an often neglected topic

Chapter 4

Graham Darby, 'Garibaldi – Luck of Judgement', *History Review*, **September 2011**
A succinct account and assessment of Garibaldi's contribution to Italian unification

Lucy Riall, *Garibaldi: Invention of a Hero* **(Yale University Press, 2008)**
A fascinating explanation of how Garibaldi came to be seen as a larger-than-life hero not only in Italy but in the wider world

Lucy Riall, 'Garibaldi: The First Celebrity', *History Today*, **August 2007**
An article that presents, in easily accessible form, the main ideas in Riall's *Garibaldi: Invention of a Hero*

Jasper Ridley, *Garibaldi* **(Constable, 1974)**
A 700-page biography, strong on personality and events. Despite its length, it is very readable and well worth consulting

Chapter 5

Martin Clark, *Modern Italy 1871 to the Present Day* **(Routledge, 2008)**
Chapters 1–5 are a detailed introduction to the period

Christopher Duggan, 'Nation-building in 19th-century Italy', *History Today*, **February 2002**
Excellent on the role of Crispi

F.G. Stapleton, 'Liberal Italy', *History Review*, **December 2001**
A spirited defence of the record of Italian governments after 1861

Chapter 6

Alan Farmer, 'How Italy was Unified', *History Review*, **March 2006**
A good assessment of the roles of the key players

J.A. Davis, editor, *Italy in the Nineteenth Century* **(Oxford University Press, 2001)**
A collection of sometimes difficult but always instructive essays, well worth consulting towards the end of a course on Italian unification. There are chapters on politics after 1789, Mazzini, Cavour, Garibaldi, religion, culture, the economy and the 1870–96 period

Some key books in the debate

M. Clark, *The Italian Risorgimento* **(Longman, 1998)**
Christopher Duggan, *The Force of Destiny* **(Allen Lane, 2007)**
Harry Hearder, *Italy in the Age of the Risorgimento, 1790–1870* **(Longman, 1983)**
Walter Maturi, *Interpretazioni del Risorgimento* **(Turin, 1962)**
Denis Mack Smith, *The Making of Italy* **(Macmillan, 1968) and** *Italy: A Modern History* **(University of Michigan, 1979)**
Lucy Riall, *Risorgimento* **(Palgrave Macmillan, 2009)**
G.M. Trevelyan, *Garibaldi and the Making of Italy* **(Longman, 1911)**

Index